Christmas
TRADITIONS

Christmas
TRADITIONS

True Stories that Celebrate the Spirit of the Season

EDITED BY HELEN SZYMANSKI

Aadamsmedia
AVON, MASSACHUSETTS

Published by
Adams Media, a division of F+W Media, Inc.
57 Littlefield Street, Avon, MA 02322. U.S.A.
www.adamsmedia.com

ISBN 10: 1-59869-838-9
ISBN 13: 978-1-59869-838-1

Printed in the United States of America.

J I H G F E D C B A

Library of Congress Cataloging-in-Publication Data
is available from the publisher.

This publication is designed to provide accurate and authoritative information with regard
to the subject matter covered. It is sold with the understanding that the publisher is not
engaged in rendering legal, accounting, or other professional advice. If legal advice or
other expert assistance is required, the services of a competent professional person should
be sought.

—From a *Declaration of Principles* jointly adopted by a Committee of the
American Bar Association and a Committee of Publishers and Associations

Many of the designations used by manufacturers and sellers to distinguish their product are
claimed as trademarks. Where those designations appear in this book and Adams Media
was aware of a trademark claim, the designations have been printed with initial capital
letters.

This book is available at quantity discounts for bulk purchases.
For information, please call 1-800-289-0963.

Dedication

This book is dedicated to the Spirit of Christmas.

Acknowledgments

A special thank-you is extended to the hundreds of authors who submitted their work to this book. I wish I could have found a home for each and every story. I'd also like to thank my agent, Kate Epstein; my in-house editor, Andrea Norville; everyone at Adams Media and F+W Media, Inc.; and my family, whom I dearly love. And, as always, I'd like to thank the Lord, for He has never let me down. He gives me great visions, holds my hand when I need it, and always, always believes in me.

Contents

CONTENTS

Introduction

My Christmas traditions are many. Each part of my life has brought with it beautiful traditions that I will hold close for all time.

Jesus is the number-one reason for my Christmas season, but I also have a whimsical tradition, which I love. It started when I was a child, and it's what keeps me a child at heart: my fascination with elves. I grew up in the '50s and '60s, about the time the first red-felt elf made its appearance in the branches of Christmas trees 'round the globe. I was immediately caught up in the magic. Because my siblings and I wanted the elves to know they were welcome in our home, we built elf doors and little bitty furniture for them out of bark and moss. Today, that tradition has grown. Dozens of elves now peek from nooks and crannies around my house, and these days I make wooden elf doors and sell them online at *www.theelfdoor.com*, so every child can enjoy the magic.

As Christmas approaches, I encourage everyone to remember that the season really and truly is about the Christ Child, but when it comes to creating a family tradition, I also hope that each of my readers starts at least one special magical tradition. It's that extra bit of magic that makes a routine activity—like adopting another elf or erecting another elf door—the second most-important thing that will come to mind when we remember the Christmas holiday and all of the special family traditions we've enjoyed over the years.

—*Helen Szymanski*

CHRISTMAS

TRADITIONS

"Touch the heart of a loved one this Christmas. Decorate your tree with one-of-a-kind love notes."

BY JOAN CLAYTON

Love Notes on My Tree

"I wish I could find enough words to tell you how much I love you," said my tall, dark, and handsome husband, as he held me tight in the privacy of our little apartment. I knew he worried about not being able to buy me a present, but he needn't have. Emmitt had just finished his tenure in the army and had enrolled in college on the GI Bill. We had been married only a few months, and he wanted our newlywed Christmas to be special.

"You're my present and always will be," I answered. He smiled in relief. "Come on," I said. "Let's go shopping for a tree. Maybe we'll find one we can afford."

I think the salesman guessed our financial condition when he saw us coming up the walk. "The trees have been picked over," he explained. "But, believe it or not, I have just the tree for you." A kind smile appeared on his face. "I'll sell it for one dollar."

We thanked him and hurried home with the first of many evergreens that would grace our home over the coming years. We had nothing to decorate it with, so we just sat with love-filled eyes and stared at it, listening to "I'm Dreaming of a White Christmas" playing on the radio. Emmitt looked at me and smiled. "Let's dance," he whispered, pulling me close. I thought I was in heaven.

Before Emmitt went to class the next day, he sat down and wrote a note on a little square of paper. Telling me not to look at it until Christmas, he folded the paper carefully and tied it on a bough near the top of our little evergreen. I was so taken in by his romantic gesture that I decided to do the same thing.

When Emmitt came home that night, he noticed there were two notes on the tree. The next day, he wrote another note and placed it on the tree. I did the same. By the time Christmas Eve arrived, our "love note" ornaments dressed our tree to perfection. There wasn't a couple more in love than we were that first Christmas.

When Christmas Day came, we sat together on the floor and carefully, one by one, opened our love notes. As we read them aloud to each other, we moved ever closer. Finally, I folded my last precious note and looked into his big brown eyes.

"You are God's gift to me," I said, "and that's the greatest gift I could ever receive."

I guess he could see in my eyes that I was telling the truth, because he pulled me up into his arms, swept me off my feet, and twirled me around the room happily. Wrapped in the glow of our special love, we danced to the kitchen, where we had a Christmas dinner of tuna sandwiches. To someone else, that might have been a disappointment, too, but to us it was a feast!

After Christmas, I took the notes off the tree and put them in a box for safekeeping. The next Christmas, we added new notes to the tree. At the end of the season, I carefully packed them into a bigger box.

By the time our boys came along, our Christmas tree was brimming with love notes to each other and to our precious children. It was our love tree and it was perfect. As soon as the boys were old enough to understand, they scribbled on bits of paper and hung their notes on the tree, too! As they grew, their notes became priceless sentiments:

Mommy, will you marry me when I grow up?
Daddy, can we go rock hunting for Christmas?
Mommy, I love you because you pillow-fight with me.
Daddy, I like the way you throw balls.
Mommy, do you want a dog that I saw outside for Christmas?
Daddy, you're the best daddy!

Inevitably, our boys grew up, married, and had babies of their own. Though our family nucleus has changed, some things are too precious to set by the wayside. Today, our grandchildren write love notes to hang on our special tree, too.

Now, on Christmas, as the whole family sits in a circle around the Christmas tree, Jody, my tall, dark, and handsome grandson—very much like the tall, dark, and handsome man I married so long ago—starts our family tradition. As I look around the circle, the song "I'm Dreaming of a White Christmas" plays in my heart and I dance with Emmitt again. Pulling the first note from the tree, Jody unties the ribbon, unfolds the paper, and smiles. "To Granddad, from Jody," he reads. Smoothing the paper, he turns to face his grandfather. "Granddad," he says proudly, "I'm so thankful you passed on a name to be proud of to my father, who in turn passed it on to me!"

Emmitt beams as Jody, an ear-to-ear grin on his face, returns to his place in the circle, and then one of our granddaughters stands. As she begins to unfold her first note, Emmitt's eyes meet mine across the circle. I think he is listening to the same song that plays in my head. My eyes tell him he is God's gift to me, the greatest gift I could ever receive, and I know by the way he gazes back at me that he knows it's still true.

"Remind Santa to always use his magical, special wrapping paper—never the same paper you use for other Christmas gifts."

BY DONNA SUNDBLAD

𝔊anta's 𝔠all

Grace peeked in on her four oldest children. Moonlight crept across the two sets of bunk beds, highlighting their angelic faces. In the six short years, since they'd moved into this two-bedroom house, their family had swollen from three to seven. The eldest, now ten, still believed in Santa, and Grace longed to keep the magic of Christmas intact for as long as possible.

Christmas Eve was tomorrow—she was running out of time.

Taking advantage of the hour she had left before it was time to feed the baby, Grace tiptoed to the basement door and followed the steep wooden stairs downward. Discarded living room furniture from her mother-in-law's apartment cluttered the area to her right. Her ringer-washer, dryer, and chest freezer stood on the left, and straight ahead—hidden beneath the old chenille bedspread—was a mountain of Santa gifts.

Grace sighed and rubbed her tired eyes. Times like this made her wish Howie didn't have to work nights, but it was the extra money that helped make ends meet and allowed them to provide a Christmas far beyond what either of them had ever experienced as children.

The sump pump clicked, startling her back to the task at hand. She moved to the hoard of Christmas gifts, mounded against the unpainted cement wall in the corner, removed the bedspread, plucked the Shrinking Violet doll from the melee, and centered it on the old oak canning table. From the top shelf of canned goods, she grabbed her stash of Santa wrapping paper and set to work.

Grace always made sure the wrapping paper she used on Santa's gifts was different from the paper she used to wrap gifts for her family. The white tissue paper, sprinkled with tiny metallic stars, was part of the magic. Last year, ten-year-old Donna had noticed a smattering of the little stars on the floor and told the other children it was magic stardust that helped Santa get from the ground to the sleigh on the rooftop in houses like theirs without a fireplace. Grace smiled at the innocence of childhood.

Racing against the clock, Grace wrapped as quickly as she could. Before long, the pile of presents she had wrapped was larger than the unwrapped pile. But, one glance at her wristwatch and she knew—she was running out of time. Scooping up the remaining wrapping paper, she reached up to place it on a high shelf. A wave of panic swept over her, as she realized how little of the star-studded paper remained. She stared at the remnant in her hand with a sinking feeling. A quick glance at the stack of gifts confirmed her worst fears. She didn't have enough paper for the bigger gifts.

Now what? How could she get away on Christmas Eve to buy more gift wrap, without the kids wondering where she was going, or worse, wanting to come along?

As she fed three-month-old Mary, Grace continued to fret. *What was she to do about the Santa gifts?*

The problem was the three big gifts for the oldest girls. The secretaries would help the girls organize their things, and the fold-down desk doubled as a chalkboard.

How in the world would she wrap them?

The following day, as the children bounced around the house with excitement, Grace waited nervously for Howie to wake up.

"Mom," Donna called. "We need to frost the cookies. Santa's coming tonight!" She laced her fingers and drew her hands under her chin, excitement dancing in her eyes.

Grace groaned. She'd forgotten the cookies! *How on earth would she get out for wrapping paper before the stores closed?*

Just then, four-year-old Gail squealed from the window. Her angelic face turned toward her family, the excitement evident in her eyes.

"It's snowing," she shouted.

Grace hurried to the window. Big white snowflakes drifted lazily to the ground, where they collected like a heavy wet blanket. She had wanted a white Christmas as much as the children, but as she stared out the window, she fought tears. Pulling herself together for their sake, she turned toward her family and smiled.

"Well, looks like we'll have a white Christmas after all."

"Maybe we'll see reindeer tracks," five-year-old Micky said hopefully.

"And sleigh tracks on the roof!" Donna added.

"Let's go frost those cookies," Grace called, as cheerfully as she could.

Within minutes, the children were sitting around the table in front of four mixing bowls. The girls chattered about what they hoped to get for Christmas, while one-year-old Mark sat on the stepstool beside Grace, waiting to dip his finger in the frosting. After Grace divided the powdered-sugar frosting between the bowls and added food coloring, she dumped colored sugar crystals onto plates, and let the children start decorating. She had initiated this cookie decorating as a new family tradition, and she looked forward to it as much as they did. But all she could think about right now was Santa's wrapping paper.

Suddenly, Grace smiled. She had an idea.

That evening, the kids climbed into their pajamas without argument. Afterward, they sat in the living room chatting happily and starring at the few family presents already tucked beneath the tinsel-covered tree. They hardly looked up when the phone in the hall rang.

Grace tried to keep a straight face, as she said hello into the receiver. A moment later, she was looking into the living room at her eldest child.

"Donna," she called. "It's for you."

The chatter of children's voices vanished. They all looked at their sister in surprise.

"For me?" Donna asked.

Grace nodded and Donna hurried to the phone. Before she handed the receiver to her daughter, Grace covered the mouthpiece with her hand and whispered, "It's Santa!"

Donna's eyes grew wide. "Hello?" she said in a voice full of wonder. "Yes . . ."

Micky and Gail crowded into the small hallway, staring at their sister. "What's he saying?" Micky asked.

"Oh no . . . okay," Donna said. "I'll ask my mom. Hold on."

Donna placed her hand over the receiver, mimicking her mother. "Mom," she whispered, "Santa had an accident. The reindeer made a quick turn, and a few presents fell out of the sleigh and the wrapping paper tore. He wants to know if we can leave him some wrapping paper along with the cookies."

"How much does he need?"

"How much do you need, Santa?" Donna asked. She listened for a moment, her eyes growing round. "He has three *big* presents. One for me, one for Micky, and one for Gail!"

Grace smiled. Then she nodded. "Yes. We can do that."

"Be it sugar cookies or a certain box of chocolates, every family has a special treat they love to indulge in during the holidays."

BY CHERYL K. PIERSON

Maybe It's a Pony

I have always enjoyed Christmas the most out of anyone in our family. There has never been any doubt. Being the youngest of three—my two sisters on the verge of entering their teenage years when I was born—made that fact indisputable. By the time I was able to talk, to understand buying gifts for others, I couldn't keep my enthusiasm to myself.

I also couldn't keep a secret.

My dad always seemed to be able to wheedle the surprise out of me. It started as a game, turning to serious business somewhere along the line—but I was never quite sure where, or how. Dad never came right out and *asked* what I had gotten him for Christmas. He was far too clever for that.

"We're wrapping presents!" I would announce.

Dad would cock a dark brow as if there might be a problem with that. "Before you do," he'd say seriously, "remember, my favorite color is blue."

"Oh, it's blue, all right," I assured him.

8

"Dark or light?"

"Real light."

"Like the sky or like a robin's egg?" This seemed important for him to know, and I felt it would be all right. After all, there were lots of blue objects in the world; he just wanted to know the color—that's all.

"Blue like a robin's egg."

He'd pretend to be in deep thought for a long moment. Then, "Well, it's *harder* than a robin's egg, isn't it?"

"Oh, yes. It's hard." After I thought about it, though, it seemed prudent to warn him. "But, it *will* break."

Again, the thoughtful pause. "It will?"

I could see I needed to keep him from worrying. "Well, it won't break like a robin's egg, but it *is* glass."

It was usually at this point that Mom or one of my older sisters would try to end the conversation. I'd notice Mom giving Dad a dark look; one that seemed to say, "You should be ashamed of yourself."

Dad would smile and walk away—not the least bit worried about whatever Mom was trying to shame him with. If Mom weren't around, one of my sisters would take me by the hand and glare at Dad, admonishing me as they hustled me back to the bedroom, where we were wrapping. "Don't tell him what it is! You *always* tell what it is!" Ever since I had learned to talk, that was fast becoming a tradition.

As we wrapped the blue glass ashtray, they explained to me—or *tried* to explain—how Dad was tricking the answers out of my eager five-year-old mouth. At fifteen and seventeen, they'd been down this road before. But at my age, I didn't stop to wonder what made them so wise.

Once the gifts were wrapped and set carefully under the tree, my resolve strengthened. There were only four more days until Christmas. Surely, *surely* I could keep a secret for four more days.

I began to be watchful, wary, and thoughtful when Dad started talking about presents. He'd lean back in his easy chair, a cigarette in hand, Chet Huntley and David Brinkley coming into our home for the nightly news. But before they could get warmed up, Dad said, "I sure hope ol' Santa's good to me this year. There are a few things I've really been wanting."

"What?" I asked. My sisters and Mom braced themselves for round two.

In all seriousness, he looked at me and said, "I'd really like to have a pony."

"Me, too!" I exclaimed.

"But, if I don't get *that* . . . I'd like to have a couple of boxes of chocolate-covered cherries and maybe some warm long johns and a new ashtray for my desk."

My eyes went wide. He *was* getting a new ashtray! I also knew Mom had planned to get him some chocolate-covered cherries, another long-standing tradition. But the long johns and the pony—I wasn't sure of those.

I doubted seriously that a pony would come to our family. I had asked before, and it hadn't happened yet. He was going to be disappointed, just as I had been. But, maybe, if he knew he was getting the ashtray, he wouldn't be so sad about the pony.

"Well, you're going to love your present, 'cause—"

"Cheryl!" the other three Moss women chorused in warning.

Dad leaned forward, a questioning look on his face. "I am? Why?"

"Because you just will," Mom said, giving him one of "those" looks over the top of my head.

Yet, somehow, he always managed to get it out of me. Sometimes, my answers to his questions gave it away; once, I blurted it out when the others weren't around. It was a secret I was sorry I'd told, for his sake, and sorry I didn't keep, for my own. I was in anguish over my lack of willpower.

After that, I became stronger in my resolve, and the tradition of Dad trying to find out his gifts—and me telling him too much—was broken. He had accomplished what he'd tried to teach me: that sometimes, even though it's hard to wait, the joy of the surprise is better than the certainty of the gift.

Forty-plus years later, he was still teasing me. I brought him a wrapped box of chocolate-covered cherries the first week of December 2007. When I handed them to him, he asked, "Now, what could this be?"

"Maybe it's a pony," I responded dryly.

He gently shook the box, knowing exactly what was in it. Chocolate-covered cherries are the only things that come in a box that size. "No, I don't think so," he answered thoughtfully, not cracking a smile. "Will it break?" He was up to his old tricks again.

"You better just open it," I told him with a smile, "and *see* what it is."

He tore into the present, thinking he knew for sure what he was opening. The only question in his mind was milk chocolate or dark. But as he pulled the paper away, I knew I had him. He held the box up, squinting in the late afternoon sun.

"Well, I'll be," he muttered, as surprised as if it *had* been a pony. "*Peppermint-flavored* chocolate-covered cherries. I didn't know they made such a thing!"

And I hadn't told him, either!

"Hang holly leaves above the doorway, windows, and mirrors of your home as a symbol of better times heading your way."

BY ROSEMARY GOODWIN

Holly Berry Dreams

I was a shy little girl, four years old, and home was a lovely, albeit primitive, thatched English cottage in a small country village.

Overhead, RAF squadrons of Spitfire fighter planes buzzed our homes as they headed from the local aerodromes toward their targets, and huge Lancaster bombers groaned, their engines straining to get their bulk up into the black clouds of war. When sirens wailed to warn us of incoming enemy planes, we dove under the stairs to keep safe from falling timbers. We'd crawl out at the "all-clear" sound, blinking in the bright light like nearsighted moles emerging from their holes.

No toys were made during this period, but we were children of the war and knew no other life, so toys weren't missed—much. I did yearn for a baby carriage for my dolls, but Mum explained it was out of reach. Materials were devoured by the war machine. Even green paint was difficult to find in civilian shops. Green paint colored the tanks and Jeeps.

Instead of toys, my joys were culled from discovering green-frilled white snowdrops in the snow and making a posy of fragrant violets for Mum. Every day, I looked in the hedgerows and filled a basket with brown eggs collected from the chicken nest-boxes found in the old Gypsy cart parked in our neighbor's meadow. Mr. Redwood, an asthmatic old man who coughed long and loud into a yellowed handkerchief, didn't mind if I spent hours sitting on that cart driving a make-believe horse down fantasy roads, either. That imaginary caravan drive was my escape from the bleak rationed days of 1944.

Winter meant long, dreary cold days spent in itchy wool hats and gloves, while we kept our fingers crossed that it wouldn't rain. Puddles would make the cardboard covering the holes in our shoes fall apart. Darkness arrived early, so we made tea by the light of an oil lamp, lit only after the blackout curtains were drawn.

On rainy days, Mum took a shoebox from the shelf in her wardrobe and placed it on the table in front of the crackling fire. We made toast by spearing a slice of bread on the end of a long fork, letting the flames turn the bread into a tanned delight to be covered in butter. As we feasted, Mum lined up old photographs of a man. Sometimes, he wore a suit, other times an army uniform.

"This is your daddy," she said gently. "He'll be home some day when the war is over."

I was the proud owner of an ancient alphabet book, which I shared with my playmates. The drawing of "B is for balloon" always caused us to wish for one on a shooting star—or was it a searchlight casting about the sky for enemy planes? Looking up with pleading eyes, I asked Mum if Father Christmas could bring us a balloon this year for Christmas.

"No," Mum said, "there will be no balloons for children until after the war."

As the holiday neared, Mum and I rode our bicycles to Granddad's house to gather branches of holly from his garden. We pedaled home with smiles on our faces and prickly red-berried branches jammed into the baskets on the front of our bikes. For a little while, it felt as if there was no such thing as war. According to Mum, we were carrying out an age-old tradition.

"All of the other trees in the woods have no leaves in the dead of winter," she explained. "The holly has lovely green leaves." Then she grinned happily. "It means that better times are coming!"

In our small living room, I stood on a chair to place a small branch of holly over the top of each mirror and picture frame—then I climbed down and admired my work. Mum helped me nail holly over the doorway, too.

She took coils of crêpe paper out of the pantry—faded now over time—but still pretty. Together, we twisted the paper into swirls and hung it from the corners of the room to the center of the ceiling. Using a wartime recipe, we made plum pudding and, because Mum had saved a few coupons, we managed to buy some icing sugar for our Christmas cake.

We sang carols all around the village that evening and with rosy cheeks went willingly to bed. Mum hung an old wool stocking on the headboard of my bed, and kissed me, offering hope for happy dreams on this wonderful night. No bombs dropped that Christmas Eve. It really was a silent night.

I lay in bed wondering. *What on earth will Father Christmas bring me?* There wasn't much for him *to* bring. Would his sleigh get shot down? Praying for his safety, I was soon peacefully asleep.

"Happy Christmas, Mummy," I yelled the next morning, as I jumped on her bed. "Can I open my presents now?"

"Of course, dear," she said happily. "Get your stocking first, and then I have a surprise for you."

I emptied the stocking on her soft comforter. Out poured candy, walnuts, a coloring book, and an orange—a rare treat!

"Aunt Joan has managed to find some coloring pencils, which she'll bring over later," Mum said, as she watched me take in all of my treasures with wide eyes.

I looked up at her then, remembering. "What's your surprise?"

"Let's go downstairs and see," she said. Without waiting for her, I bounded down the stairs, two at a time.

There, in the middle of the kitchen table, sat a parcel wrapped in brown paper and tied up with string. I pulled on the string and tore it open. I felt as rich as the richest child in the world.

"Oh Mummy!" I cried. "I wished for a doll carriage, and you got me one!"

My hands shook as I touched my gift. It was the shoebox from Mum's wardrobe. Two meat skewers pierced the ends, and four empty cans of shoe polish were added on the bottom as wheels. A small rag doll looked up at me from a tiny pillow made out of one of Mum's hankies. Tears ran down my cheeks, as I pulled my doll carriage along by its string, saying "This is the best-est present I've ever had!"

It was the best present I had ever gotten, and it still is. Every time my children and I hang Christmas holly over the pictures in our family room, I remember it well. Memories flood back then, as I, like my mother before me, help my children hang holly around the doorways and over the mirrors and windows.

And, as I help small hands reach the highest points, I remember my mother's voice explaining why the holly has lovely green leaves.

"It means that better times are coming," I whisper, as Mum had done so long ago. I smile, as I look at my children, for I know Mum was right. Better times did come for us, and I know even better times are coming for my own children.

"Share the joy of Christmas each year by donating the gift of a book to the local library, or the gift of your time to a literacy program."

BY ANNA VON REITZ

The Gift of Knowledge

It was 1975. I was a college student looking for a cause. The tide of Vietnamese War refugees was hitting American shores, and the call had gone out for volunteers—literacy volunteers. People were needed to teach other adults how to read and, if necessary, how to speak English. I signed up.

Sixteen weeks later, I emerged a full-fledged instructor, armed with alphabet cards, immense goodwill, and a bleary-eyed idea of what I was doing. I waited for my first student, imagining it would be someone from Southeast Asia. She turned out to be a grandmother from Louisiana.

She was eighty years old and had spent her entire life cooking for other people, training their dogs, childrearing, and accomplishing other domestic miracles. Her name was Mabel Mae Snyder, and she was scared of me. When I arrived at her house, I stood in the foyer and stared up at her. She was as black as night, six feet tall, and from the look of her forearms, could still climb a rope, but she peered at me with obvious terror.

"Are you Mrs. Snyder?" I asked tentatively.

"That's me," she answered, nodding her head slowly.

"You want to read?"

"I do."

It sounded like a marriage vow.

"I was just making some tea," she said, momentarily forgetting that she was afraid of me. "Would you like some?"

I nodded.

"I'm eighty years old, and I don't know how to read," she confessed. "I can understand signs for the door and where the washroom is, but nothing strung together. Can you help me?"

"Sure," I said confidently. "Do you know the alphabet?"

"Not really," she said softly.

We spent the evening on the letter A.

"Whew!" Mrs. Snyder remarked, when we were finished. "Are all the letters like this?"

"Only the vowels," I assured her.

"And how many of them are there?" She rolled her eyes back apprehensively.

"Five main ones—and a switch hitter."

Mabel Mae understood baseball, and I knew we had found common ground. I smiled. "What's the first thing you want to read, Mrs. Snyder?"

"Oh, call me Mabel!" she insisted, and then looked thoughtful. "A storybook," she said, "one with pretty pictures."

That spring, we took a field trip. We faced the librarian together. I explained that Mabel was going to take out some books for her grandchildren, which was only half a lie, because by that time, I'd learned something else. Mabel wanted to read stories to her grandchildren.

By December, she was ready.

"I got to get my daughter to come visit me," she confided. Her handsome face twisted with pain. "But she's ashamed of me."

"What about your son?" I asked.

"He's in prison," she whispered. "Been there for fourteen years."

Almost as soon as she said that, there was a knock on the door. Mabel opened the door and screamed.

"Lord! Lord! It's my Teddy!"

There, in the doorway, stood her son. He was a tall handsome man, with his mother's nose and smile. He threw his arms around her, and closed his eyes, and, for a few moments, there was no sound from Mabel at all, as if the shock of seeing him had taken her breath away.

On the way home that night, I stopped in the middle of the street. Overcome by the events of the day, I howled. "Good Lord! Now her daughter needs a knock on the head!" I wondered if her daughter, Lena, who had left home years ago and married an attorney, would ever come around. It would be wonderful for Mabel to see her grandchildren for Christmas, but it seemed too much to ask.

The next morning was Christmas Eve. I was surprised when the phone rang. It was Mabel's voice on the other end.

"You have to drive us to Milwaukee," she pleaded. "My daughter fell down the stairs last night and hit her head."

Be careful what you ask for, I thought as I hung up the phone, feeling a little guilty. An hour later, we piled into Mabel's 1960 Studebaker Lark and were on our way.

When Lena opened the door, she flushed angrily and then frowned.

"What are you doing here?" She snapped at Mabel. Then she pointed toward Teddy. "And what trash have you dragged in with you?"

"Your brother is your brother," Mabel snapped back. "He has the same blood as you."

Though Lena continued to scowl, she finally opened the door.

"Well, don't just stand there," she spat.

Just then Lena's husband walked in. Lena glanced at him and then turned to me. In a much nicer tone she said, "I don't believe I've met you."

"She's my reading teacher," Mabel responded in my behalf.

Lena's mouth dropped open. "*Your* reading teacher?"

"Yes."

"You are learning to read—*at your age*?"

"I already did learn. Now, it's just practice."

Lena stared at her mother. "You can read?"

"And write more than my name," Mabel concluded fiercely.

Lena's husband cleared his throat and ended the standoff.

"Mother Snyder?" he asked gently.

"What is it?" she asked, without taking her eyes from her daughter's.

"Don't you want to see the children?"

Within seconds, he was leading Mabel up the stairs, leaving Lena, Teddy, and me, to continue staring at one another in silence.

Unable to hold the truth in any longer, I glared at Lena. "I have hated you all week."

Lena frowned. "Why?"

"Because you're not proud of her."

"Proud of a *washerwoman,* who never went to school?"

"She made sure *you* graduated."

Lena stared at me for a long moment. As we glared at each other, her eyes filled with tears. Turning, Lena ran upstairs, suddenly desperate to find her mother.

Later that night, Mabel sat with a grandchild on each knee, reading a story about a baby, a wandering star, and Three Wise Men. She read every word flawlessly and with feeling.

Every year since, I read the same glorious story at Christmastime, sharing it with family and friends, and whoever else will listen. And I remember Mabel Snyder. I may have taught her how to read, but she taught me to value what I had taken for granted, including the ability to read the Scripture for myself. Every year, my family donates a beautiful picture book to the public library in Mabel's honor.

> *"Helping distribute goods to families in need during the holidays can be one of the most cherished of memories and traditions."*

BY DIANE SERIO

Mrs. Claus

For as long as I can remember, the faculty and staff have passed an inconspicuous manila envelope around our elementary school asking for donations to the holiday fund. So many of our families were in great need of food and warm clothing for their children. As their teachers, we did not want them to go without during the holidays.

We volunteered the names of families who'd just arrived in America and could not afford field trips, birthday treats, or winter coats; those whose fathers had lost jobs or whose mothers had welcomed new babies; and those who simply could not afford clothes for each day in the week. We knew these children well. We watched them—too eager for breakfast to be served, embarrassed by no birthday treats to share, or with pants too small to reach their shoes. We knew them, and every impulse we had was to make the need less, the days more comfortable, the holiday more joyous.

Selected families were asked if they could use help with the necessities each holiday season. Notes were taken on sizes and lists were given to shoppers. Happy to make holiday wishes come true, we shopped for underwear, boots, and sweaters and, feeling surprises were just as necessary, always included a game or small toy in the boxes, too.

The teachers' lounge became a workshop, where gift-wrappers took turns preparing beautiful packages. They were all loaded into large black bags and left for the delivery group to take to their homes before winter break.

I have wrapped, shopped, or delivered each year. One particular year, we had fewer volunteers and a snowstorm stranded some gifts that needed to be delivered the day before break. Because I recognized the name on the tag as a child I'd had in my class years earlier, I was reluctant. Part of the magic of the holiday fund was the anonymity. But, someone had to do it.

I loaded up my trunk and crept slowly through whirling snow on whitewashed streets. The apartment was part of a large complex. The family lived on the third floor, in a one-bedroom apartment, with another family. The snow was plowed into hills on the lot. I could only handle one bag at a time against the wind.

The front-door locks were broken. The doorbell summoned a woman from the apartment above, who wrapped herself in a sweater and spoke hurriedly to her children, "Shh, go, now. Inside!" She was tiny and tired. Her clothes were layered, and I wondered if they had enough heat.

Her daughter, with a voice so small and an accent that added vowels to the end of each word, yelled again to her mother, and asked who was at the door. Her nervous mother lifted the bag, looking back to the closed door above, trying to keep our secret.

"There are two more bags," I said, copying her hushed tones, so the kids couldn't hear me and recognize my voice. "I'll be right back."

The wind and cold air tossed my hair into my face, covering my eyes, as I waded through snow on the drifted walkway back to my car.

The woman waited at the door, one hand waving her children back behind her, the other reaching for the bag I handed her. Her cheeks were rosy from the wind, and her eyes were filled with tears.

"This is too much," she sobbed. "Too much." Wiping away tears of joy, with the back of her hand, she looked up at me. I swallowed hard. Gratitude like that is hard to find. I said nothing, handed her the last of the bags, and watched as she surveyed her entire holiday. All they would receive was in three large bags. I knew the check I had added to that manila envelope was well worth this.

She lugged the bag up two flights to their apartment, while I waited down below. I could hear voices, whispers in Polish, wafting down. On the last trip, her daughter, my former student, appeared in the stairwell. She was surprised, but waved and blushed to see her former teacher standing in the lobby of her home. Her mother spoke harshly, and she instantly backed up.

As I was leaving, a gust of wind carried her mother's voice over the balcony. "You see," she said to her children, "only in America can your teacher be your Santa Claus, too."

"Make the holiday a little warmer for someone in need. Join the local soup kitchen and ladle up a few hearty smiles along with the soup."

BY ANGIE LEDBETTER

Modern-Day Drummer Boy

Trouble seemed to follow my young nephew, Tony, like a shadow. The way I looked at it: Others walked to the beat of a different drum, but Tony—poor thing—was the drummer. And he banged his drum in a loud offbeat cadence.

The school principal had quit listening to his explanations.

"I don't know why I get sent to the office so much," Tony said to his mother after she had received another call from school.

My sister, Marion, rubbed her temples, as a tear slid down her face. Her heart broke for her son, as did mine. It was with a heavy heart that I watched her pull Tony close, and pat his head reassuringly.

"Oh, Tony," she whispered, "I wish everyone could see the beautiful person you are inside."

"It's okay," Tony insisted, as he raced outside to play, the incident already forgotten.

Marion smiled, as she watched him through the window. In her heart of hearts, she knew he was a gift to the world. "They just don't know it yet," she said softly.

The counselors and doctors had assured us Tony was in perfect health. In fact, at age three, he had placed in the genius IQ level on standardized testing. They speculated that his youth, a high-geared mind, and ADHD were working together to his disadvantage.

But what the doctors and specialists didn't know, and could never diagnose, was Tony's heart of gold. With old-fashioned discipline, lots of love, and a full schedule of activities, Marion prayed the constant disapproval and cutting remarks Tony received from outside the family circle didn't damage his self-esteem.

One of Tony's most attentive activities was helping the elderly in his neighborhood. He did whatever he could to make their day brighter. He also had a way with babies and young children. Because Tony didn't see color, age, condition, or differences in people, he was also drawn to people with disabilities. Despite the negative attention he attracted, he was actually very happy. The only thing that seemed to get him down was the fact that he was still sleeping with a swatch of cloth—all that was left of his baby blanket.

"Nanny, I think it's time for me to give up my 'bobadee,'" he said one December day, as he played board games with my children.

I looked at him closely. "I thought you liked to have it when you went to bed."

Tony offered me a lopsided grin. "Yeah, I do," he said wistfully. "But some of the guys at school said only babies sleep with blankets."

"We both know not to listen to what other people say," I reminded him.

"Yeah . . . but this time . . . maybe they're right."

I could tell by the determined look on his face that it was bothering him quite a bit. "Well, think about it and you'll come up with an answer," I said, as reassuringly as I could. I knew giving up his security blanket would be hard.

As Christmas approached, unusually cold weather hit the Gulf Coast. Temperatures dropped below freezing. Both my sister and

I, and our families, were regular helpers at the men's shelter and weren't surprised when we were summoned to cook for the extra crowds trying to get out of the cold. Tony was always ready to serve spaghetti, pour drinks, or just visit with the guys, as he called the homeless men.

Driving home from serving gumbo one night, Tony reminded me he was ready to give up his blanket.

"Nanny," he said, "I've thought about giving up my bobadee—like you said—and I'm ready."

I looked in my rearview mirror and stared at him, as he and my son Josh poked each other in fun. "What do you want to do with it?" I asked, as we passed St. Agnes Catholic Church.

Tony glanced out the window and stared at the manger scene. "I wish I could give it to Baby Jesus," he said wistfully, rubbing his bobadee against his cheek. "It's so cold outside."

Tears blinded my vision as I looked at Tony's expectant face. I asked if he understood that once he gave the blanket away, he couldn't take it back again.

Tony smiled at me. "I think He *really* needs it more than I do." Then he shrugged. "Anyway, it's almost His birthday and I don't have anything else to give Him."

I wiped my misty eyes and turned the van around. In seconds, we were parked alongside the curb near the huge crèche. For a moment, we all stared at the proud marble Joseph as he stood guard over Baby Jesus among the barn animals in the skimpy wooden structure. Then our eyes traveled to the beautiful Mother Mary bent over her baby.

I eyed the fence surrounding the stable and shook my head. "Boys," I said, "say a prayer my old arm can make it over the fence, okay?" As I wadded the fabric into a small ball, the boys giggled. "Please deliver this package for me," I prayed aloud. Rolling down the window, I lobbed Tony's bobadee over the fence.

We held out breath as the material sailed over the fence and then plummeted toward earth. Oh no! Tony's prize possession was falling about two feet shy of its target. My heart fell, and I closed my eyes. There would be no second tries.

"Nanny, look!" Tony screeched. I opened my eyes just as a gust of wind picked up the material and guided it to the tiny outstretched hand of Baby Jesus. We cheered, as Tony's gift draped over the Christmas Infant as if it had belonged there.

As we drove away, grinning like fools, the first strains of the perfect song for this perfect occasion floated from the radio. And as the boys *pa-rum-pa-pum-pummed* in the backseat to the beat of "The Little Drummer Boy," I found new significance in the lyrics. The little drummer and Tony had so much in common. They both walked to a different beat, and they both had beautiful gifts to share.

*"Christmas is a time to come together
as a community to share bounty
and harvest, and to acknowledge the
love we have for one another."*

BY ELAINE K. GREEN

Observations from the Edge:
Christmas on the Lower Nine

I grew up in the Ninth Ward—more precisely, the Lower Ninth Ward of New Orleans, Louisiana—an area few people knew. During the '50s, it was the best-kept secret on the planet. My house nestled near the foot of the old Florida Avenue Bridge, in the last thicket of dwellings, before the city screeched to a stop at the parish line. I lived at the brink—the naked outer limits, the last community, the last street at the tail end of the world.

A shallow canal gurgled in front of my home. Most evenings my parents crawfished in it, exchanging stories and events of the day. I eavesdropped on their adult chatter, drank from their wisdom, and admired the way their heads nodded in loving accord beneath oversized straw hats. The canal often yielded a plentiful bounty and by nightfall we dined on succulent crawdaddies prepared to perfection by my mother's hands.

Christmas Day was an especially grand time of the year, because the neighbors on our block always gathered for our annual levee meet. Mom would spend the precious days just before the meet preparing her signature oyster dressing and coconut pecan pralines. We looked forward to Miss Coolie's sweet potato tarts and Papa Dan's homemade peach brandy.

On Christmas morning, Mom and I scaled the levee with our offerings, while Dad lingered behind putting the finishing touches on the roast turkey. From our vantage point high atop the world, we'd spy him whistling his way up the sidewalk and wave him over to join us. By that time, neighbors had already begun to gather, each armed with a dish to share: southern fried chicken, sugar snap peas, red beans and rice, corn, and candied yams. We'd gaze down at our little house and admire what was essentially two recycled army huts sandwiched together. They had been made available to veterans who couldn't afford housing after World War II. My mother had transformed those huts into a paradise. Her ambrosial azaleas rivaled the opulent greenery that lined the lush Garden District of uptown New Orleans, and pungent mint leaves from her garden garnished our lemonade.

The Lower Ninth Ward, though not on the scenic circuit, served as a perpetual oasis of enjoyment for me. Each of us had a special allegiance to the levee. We depended on it to shield us from the menacing waters of Lake Pontchartrain—a lake that was usually placid and inviting, but life-threatening during hurricane season. It also provided a peaceful refuge, where weary hands plucked buttercups and played cards in the evening cool, after a hard day of labor. These were hands that engaged in fair dealings, a decent day's work for a meager wage, hands that tended families and communities, hands that tore tender branches from wild magnolia trees to quell my youthful unruliness.

At Christmastime, we dressed the levee for the occasion. Blood red poinsettias lined her walkway interspersed with tiny white candles. It was a strikingly untraditional scene, the temperate Southern climate so unlike the greeting cards we received in the mail, which were dotted with snow and frostbitten faces.

Christmas was usually bright and sunny, and we frolicked in its warmth. It was a special time to be thankful for close friendships and to look forward to the New Year with gratitude and expectancy. While some neighbors danced with abandon to Uncle Jake's fitful fiddling, others snoozed as balmy breezes gently moved through their hair. Times were rough and jobs were hard to come by. Still, we were grateful for the little we had because that little became a lot when we shared it with each other.

It seemed futile to explain our idyllic existence to outsiders. How could I illustrate to detractors how serenely our lives flowed despite our meager incomes or how Lower Niners often exchanged chores for food throughout the year to make ends meet? They'd never understand why gentle neighbors would slaughter hogs and chickens and lay out a bountiful table not just for their own family, but for the whole community to enjoy, or how we dressed for dinner, the women adorned with fresh-cut flowers in their hair, the men scrubbed and crisp in their starched white shirts, while aunts and uncles shielded us, scolded us, and held us dear.

I remember how we basked in those Christmases on the levee, searching for four-leaf clovers, my dad doling out quarters to each kid lucky enough to find one. The gifts we exchanged weren't fancy store-bought fare, but jellies, preserves, and other homegrown foods made by our own hands in our own kitchens—something to warm not just the belly but the hungry heart. At sunset, we each carried a lighted candle down to the levee, extinguishing it as we departed, each to our own homes.

Many years have passed since that time. Some time ago, Dad and I returned to New Orleans and drove near the Florida Canal. The little bridge near the levee was barely operational, the canal now enclosed and covered with grass. "You must salvage the beauty from things," I recalled Dad saying, "and then add your special touch to them." As we traversed the narrow strip to the levee, the proud heads of many delicate buttercups danced daintily at my feet. I could still envision the tiny Christmas lights flickering before my eyes, as well as the faces of our neighbors who held them.

Dad plucked a lone flower and brushed it against my cheek. "Let's look for four-leaf clovers," he suggested, jingling the coins in his pocket. We looked across the great expanse and observed our little wooden home, looking forlorn, retaining other occupants now. I felt blessed to have shared many Christmases there and to have been a part of those special moments when time stood still.

Today our house is gone, washed away along with everyone else's. But not everything was taken. My memories are still intact. Nothing—not even Hurricane Katrina—could ever wash away the memories we shared on the Lower Nine.

*"Place an elf door in your house
and let the magic begin."*

BY ALISSA MARIE POLASKI

If You Believe in Magic

When I was a child, my parents went to great measures to instill a certain kind of magic in our lives. Our house was a haven for all things mythical. Our days were filled with fairy circles and pixie dust, and our nights with winged ponies that flew us through cookie caverns, over marshmallow mountains, and across soda-pop seas.

According to my mother, the magic had been there from the beginning of time. But for me, it all started with the sound of her voice, just above a whisper, as she told us about the magical winged ponies.

"If you let yourself believe in things bigger than you are," she said softly, the hint of a smile crossing her face, "then—I promise—you *will see* the magic."

I stared at her in awe, instinctively aware of why she had whispered. I knew if she had spoken those words aloud all the magic in the world might have disappeared right then and there. And boy, did I believe in magic then. It wasn't until much later—

when I was older and had begun to listen to the rest of the world—that I stopped believing. It would be many years before I *let* myself see the magic again and, when I did, it came in the form of something quite a bit smaller than I could have imagined.

Walking through the kitchen one spring morning, I listened in disbelief as my parents exchanged ideas on how the elf door should look.

Elf door?

"It never fails," I said, rolling my eyes. "Just when I think my family couldn't get any crazier, my parents put an elf door in the kitchen."

If they heard me they didn't seem to care. My dad was already on all fours taking measurements of a hole in the footboard. And Mom was oblivious to anything except the project at hand. Standing there in her pajamas, a silly grin on her face, she had already entered her own little world where magical creatures and fairy tales were reality. She was pleased with herself for having come up with this marvelous idea.

The elf door was red with green trim and had an itsy-bitsy golden doorknob. It was only about five or six inches in height, but to me it may as well have been ten feet tall. How was I going to explain that to my friends?

Gradually, that door and our community of elves—for that is what it eventually turned into—became a fixture in our house. No matter what time of year it was if you looked hard enough, you would find at least one or two elves cleverly tucked away in the corner of a picture frame, hanging from a chandelier, or in whatever hiding place tickled their fancy. To this day, Mom denies ever having moved them. Either way, they were there and exhibited no signs of leaving.

As summer faded into fall and fall turned into winter, I became more accustomed to the tiny fixture. In fact, I had almost forgotten it was there, until one particularly chilly winter morning when I noticed a startling new addition to the elf door.

Was that a Christmas wreath?

I squatted down to get a better look. Sure enough. Centered in the middle of the elf door was a tiny snow-covered wreath with a perky red bow. When I confronted Mom about this ridiculous discovery, she looked at me with a blank face and denied, once again, having any hand in whatever was going on.

One thing was certain—that itsy-bitsy wreath was a declaration that the Christmas season had begun, because it didn't take long for the elves to spread holiday cheer throughout our house. They came out by the dozens, invading every room with their cheeky smiles and festive outfits, and apparently reporting back to Santa every night to confirm my spot on the naughty list. At first, the whole thing seemed silly. But after a while, even I had to admit those elves really had brought a new kind of holiday cheer to our house, and I was secretly disappointed when Christmas was over.

The next year, I watched for the Christmas wreath to appear and was surprised to see several teensy-weensy presents alongside the door, in addition to the Christmas wreath. *Christmas had arrived!* The normally shy elves suddenly appeared everywhere, again.

Today, a dozen years later and a continent away, work keeps me from spending Christmas Day with my family. But every year on the first of December, my birthday gift is a plane ticket home from Mom and Dad. As soon as I walk into the kitchen, I glance at the elf door in search of the infamous Christmas wreath. As soon as I see it, all the magic that has slipped away since last year is immediately restored.

Last year, as I walked through the kitchen and out the back door with suitcase in hand, I turned and glanced at the elf door one last time. I knew it would be my last bit of magic, until I came home again, and I didn't want it to end.

Some weeks later, when my Christmas presents arrived from home, there were two gifts with notes attached that read: OPEN ME LAST.

I hurriedly opened the other gifts, then set them aside and reached for the smaller of the two packages I'd saved for last. I held back tears, as I stared at the contents of the first gift and the words my mother had spoken so very long ago echoed in my head: *If you let yourself believe in things bigger than you are, then—I promise—you will see the magic.*

I held up not one, not two, but three brand-new elves, and blinked back tears as the magic began to unfold around me. I quickly arranged the elves on the shelf overlooking my bed and reached for the last gift. It was rectangular and thick. Thinking it was a picture frame with a picture of my family in it, I smiled. When I had uncoiled a full two yards of Bubble Wrap, the red-and-green gift was finally revealed, and this time I could not contain my tears. Mom and Dad had sent me my very own elf door.

"Sometimes, simple traditions create the most lasting memories. Something as simple as an old tattered Santa hat, worn every Christmas by someone you love, will never be forgotten."

BY JANET F. SMART

The Old Santa Hat

It is sunrise on Christmas morning. The light snow, which fell during the night, glistens on the bare tree limbs. Cardinals nibble at their breakfast on the front porch. For a moment, I stand silently and stare. Then, I turn from the window, sink into my comfortable recliner, and pick up the old Santa hat lying there. I bite my lower lip and hold back the tears, as I stare at the hat. Reaching down, I pull a short gray hair from the weave in the hat. The gray hair is not mine, nor is the old Santa hat. Both were my mother's. As I clench the hair in my hand, one tear slips out and rolls down my cheek.

Mom loved Christmas. When I was a child, we made Christmas crafts together—the plump red Santa from *Reader's Digest* magazines, the pretty Christmas ornaments, and the Styrofoam Noel wall hanging. Mom passed the gift of creativity on to me. Three Christmas bags sit on the top shelf of my closet. Each bag contains handmade ornaments for my children. Every year, I add more, and when they marry, it will be my gift to them—handmade Christmas ornaments for their first tree.

I remember Mom fitting the Santa's hat over her gray hair and doing what she loved best—giving. Now, I have the hat. It isn't fancy. It's just a cheap tattered Santa hat. The ball on the end is covered in tissue paper and bells are attached to the sides with safety pins. It probably doesn't seem like much to anyone outside the family. Someone else might toss it, but not me. The cherished memories it brings to me are priceless.

I glance over my shoulder, half expecting to see Mom walk through the front door. It won't happen. She passed away long ago. But her hat is tucked away with the decorations and ornaments, and every year I retrieve it, along with the memories it holds, and place it on top of my head as Mom did. And then, with a smile on my face and a sparkle in my eyes, I pass out the presents—and I remember Mom.

I have no grandchildren yet, but when I do, I will tell them the story of this old Santa hat. I will tell them how their great-grandma put it atop her head and, with a big smile on her face and a twinkle in her eyes, passed out presents to her grandchildren on Christmas. When they say I need a fancy new hat, I will say, "Grandma doesn't need a new hat. This one may be tattered, but I will wear it proudly, until the day your daddy wears it to pass out presents to *your* children."

As the sun peaks through the curtains, voices and squeaking beds interrupt my thoughts. My family awakens to another snowy Christmas morning, and another year for me to share my mother's tradition.

I gather my composure. A soft glow flickers from the lights on our Christmas tree decorated with my handmade ornaments. Some hold memories, such as the ones I made from the old wooden spools Mom gave the kids to play with when they were little. Others will be keep-sakes in the future. I wipe away the remaining tear. As I place the old tattered Santa hat on my head, I lean forward to see who will be first to shuffle down the hallway.

"Merry Christmas, Mom," I whisper, knowing her spirit is with us on this day and always.

> *"Children in every corner of the world search for magic on Christmas Eve."*

BY EDWARD L. MELIN

A Tradition Postponed

My family traditionally attends the midnight church service on Christmas Eve and then gathers the next morning to open gifts and see what Santa brought. This was pretty standard stuff—until the year my family woke up on different continents.

The planning of this simple tradition began in 1943, as Olive and I cuddled in front of our tiny tree. It was strung with a dozen lights and decorated with four red balls. Outside of our one-bedroom apartment, snow blanketed Louisville and soot from stoves and fireplaces filled the air spoiling the mystique of the new-fallen flakes. It didn't matter though. Love and hope filled our rented space, as we dreamed of the next Christmas, when the baby Olive carried would make three. We would be joined next year by first-time grandparents, and might even have a home of our own, instead of temporary quarters near the army base. I dreamed I'd wear a Santa suit and leave gifts in my baby's stocking.

But Hitler had dreams, too, and not the kind filled with love and hope. So, on Baby Vicki's first Christmas, along with thousands of other Allied troops, I was dressed in khaki not red. I was stationed in Normandy, as a Special Services Officer for the 167th General Army Hospital, and Detachment Commander of a hospital train that ran out of Gare Saint Lazar in Paris.

The hospital didn't resemble the tree-lined street outside our two-story brick home in Amarillo, Texas. It was a sprawling tent city. Tents served as living quarters for the 500 personnel and as wards for 1,500 wounded. The chapel was a tent, not the stone building with stained-glass windows and bell tower reaching toward heaven, where Olive would worship. Four ward tents sewn together housed a theater equipped with lights from ships that had been sunk in the harbor.

In November, I mailed stocking gifts and other presents to my in-laws in Amarillo. The week before Christmas, hospital personnel—250 of us—filled the train to near capacity and carried the wounded out of the Battle of the Bulge to the *Ship of Good Hope* in Cherbourg Harbor. Then casualties slowed, and loneliness and homesickness filled the void created every time work slackened. I pictured the tree Olive described in her letters, and the red stocking hung by the fireplace, and wished I could be there.

As Special Services officer, I had the responsibility of addressing morale. *All of us* knew we would never get back those precious months away from our loved ones. *I knew* I'd never see Vicki sit up for the first time or spit cereal on her mother. But when we thought of the troops still pinned down by the Germans in the Ardennes Forest, reality resurfaced. We knew how lucky we were. Still, it was easy to feel sorry for ourselves. As I shared canned chicken and grapefruit sections sent from home with a tent mate, I longed for my mother-in-law's famous corn-bread dressing. I was in charge of morale, and my own needed work.

Our first sergeant, a Cajun from Louisiana, came forward with a plan to crack the gloom. He spoke French and had developed friendships with some of the locals. One of the women was the president of the Committee of Assistance for Prisoners of War in Tourleville. The widow of a French doctor, she also had assumed responsibility of coordinating care for families ravaged by the fighting. During her short tenure, she had identified fifty children, who had either lost both parents or their fathers were spending Christmas in a German POW camp. My hopes soared. I'd get my chance to be Santa Claus after all!

Red Santa suits were scarce, but a nurse donated a pair of white pajamas. Rit dye wasn't prevalent either, but my assistant managed to find enough to get the job done. We trimmed the red suit with cotton from surgical supply, added a tasseled cap, a wide black belt and black boots. After we glued on a beard, Santa was ready for his trip!

The children, ranging in age from six to sixteen, arrived before noon that Christmas Eve. Some of their clothing was old. Some didn't fit. Some wasn't warm enough for the season. But all of their eyes sparkled at the prospect of a break in their gloom, in much the same way ours had when we realized we had been given the chance to make a child happy on Christmas. We sang carols—theirs in French, ours in English. We shared a turkey dinner with all the trimmings in the mess tent and then went outside for the big moment. Though there was only one Santa suit, every G.I. in the compound would be passing out gifts and we were as excited as the children.

There was no snow in Tourleville that year and no sled, so Santa arrived in a cart pulled by a horse, loaded with gifts we had been able to purchase at the PX or from the locals. Most of the gifts were practical—not really what we would have chosen in better times, but fine gifts for a war-torn country in 1944. We immediately claimed a child to deliver presents to. I chose a little girl, so I could pretend I was giving the gifts to my own child so far away.

As Santa pulled his cart into sight, the children burst into laughter, surprising the rest of us. I leaned toward the woman, who had brought them, and asked what was so funny.

She smiled and whispered, "Père Noël wears white!" We laughed, too. And partied. And hoped. And dreamed, knowing that the love we experienced with these children would remain in our hearts, when we eventually returned to those whose love we shared through thoughts and letters that Christmas. And we gave thanks.

Within weeks, the Allied air forces had delivered a fatal blow to the German's fuel supply, reversing their initial success in Belgium. Additionally, the woman in charge of the children's Christmas party bicycled to the hospital to deliver a letter, which I will always treasure. The letter thanked us for the "great party given the children of POW parents and orphans of war, who will always keep in their heart and memory the souvenir of their first Christmas after the liberation of their homeland."

In February, I was treated to another letter—this one from home. In it were photos to give me a glimpse of my baby and her beautiful smile, as she ripped the paper from her Santa presents.

By Christmas 1945, my family was reunited. It may taken two years for the simple tradition Olive and I had envisioned to finally take place, but when I played Santa that year, no father could have been prouder. Every year since, as my children and grandchildren crowd around their own private Santa, I still see the faces of the children in France, who had also crowded around me. And as I tousle the hair of one of my grandchildren, I remember doing the same to another child. And as my grandchild smiles back at me, I am reminded of how those other children had smiled in much the same way, so long ago, and how those precious smiles had brightened a very lonely Christmas for a lot of GIs.

"Start a dinnertime tradition by attaching ribbons to gifts for each table setting."

BY KATHRYN ARNOLD

𝔗able 𝔊ifts

Christmas was Mom's big holiday. She even had a Christmas room that no one else was ever allowed in. That room was filled with secrets. If we were in the hall when Mom opened the door, it was an absolute must that we peak in and report any sightings. That room held all the gifts, bright-colored paper, red-satin ribbon, and exciting shiny objects that we never got to look at until Christmas.

By the time October arrived, we were already thinking about how we'd decorate the house from carpet to rafter, including the fireplace, piano, bookcases, stairway, window seat, and dining-room buffets. The buffets held multiple sets of Christmas napkins, table clothes, and crystal place markers—all the things that ladies collect for fancy dinners. But my favorite decoration was the table gifts.

On the night before Christmas, Mom set the table with her Christmas china, silver, red napkins, and silver Italian flatware, and then she arranged the spectacular centerpiece. From each plate to the center of the table ran a two-inch-wide red-satin streamer. Attached to each ribbon was an elegantly wrapped Christmas gift—one for each person coming to dinner. Mom carefully stacked the gifts one upon another, in the proper order, in the center of the table, and decorated each with red-satin bows. The pile of shiny gifts and red-satin bows created the most gorgeous centerpiece you could ever imagine.

After dinner and dessert, we waited. When the plates had been cleared, it was time! The person to Dad's left pulled the red-satin ribbon in front of him, and one gift slid from the present centerpiece and continued across the table until it had stopped in front of him. The next person pulled his ribbon, and then the next, and then the next, until at last all fourteen people seated at the table had their gifts sitting in front of them.

Then, in the same order, each person unwrapped his or her gift. Mom bought small gifts ranging from wristwatches to fine perfume or a string of pearls. We looked forward to the table gifts more than we did to the gifts beneath the tree, because when we opened the table gifts each person saw what the others received. And each time a gift was opened, we applauded while the recipient offered his or her thanks.

Later in life, in another state, my husband and I re-created this most precious tradition with our family. However, we did not have Mom's unlimited spending range, and we struggled to buy gifts small enough to fit on the table that would still allow us to have money left for our house payment in January. Just the same, this tradition was met with cheers. The following year, this tradition became too expensive for us to continue, but as each guest arrived, disappointed groans sounded from the dining room.

"Where are the table gifts?" Everyone wailed. "Where . . . how . . . you can't. . . ."

"Sorry, guys," we apologized. "But did you want a package of balloons with a pretty bow?"

We were met with stares that said, *how could you?*

As we visited before dinner, I watched the various daughters, talking to one another in serious contemplation. After dinner and dessert, one stepdaughter asked, "Would it hurt your feelings if we kept the tradition going and drew names for table gifts?"

I smiled. "Of course not!"

I loved the idea. Everybody—kids, even the men—gave a resounding cheer. It was like we had somehow cancelled Christmas, but now it had been reborn. No tradition was met with as much excitement and enthusiasm or loved to the degree this one had always been.

After the decision to draw names, the daughters saw to it that the names were drawn each year. There never was a year when someone said, "Oh, I forgot," or "I ran out of time," or "I was too busy." It was done early enough to give each of us time to shop for a gift and wrap it. And each year, the red-satin streamers were attached to multiple-colored bows, the gifts were wrapped in assorted Christmas gift-wrap, and the centerpiece was gorgeous.

The table-gift tradition celebrated its second generation twenty years ago, but then family structures changed, and some of us moved beyond driving range. You can imagine my surprise when, at a graduation party last year, my ex-husband told me that he had carried the table-gift tradition into his new family. His daughters also had carried it on in their families, and his wife continues to carry it on in her family as well.

Mom's table-gift tradition had spread from Washington, to California, Idaho, Salt Lake City, and Missouri. I hope Mom is watching. And I hope some day this tradition will travel all the way around the world and back again. That would put a nice big smile on Mom's face, and on mine.

> *"Remember to keep a special place in your heart for the Magi, who honored the Christ Child so many years ago."*

BY CYNTHIA BRIAN

Gifts of the Magi

I was lucky enough to be the eldest of five children whose parents believed in magic. We grew up on a farm in northern California and celebrated everything. Because our homestead was somewhat isolated, the family traditions that our parents created were the mainstay of my childhood.

One such holiday was Twelfth Night, or Three Wise Kings, which is celebrated on January 6. Our Swiss-Italian parents continued this celebration to honor the Magi, who followed the Star of Bethlehem to visit Baby Jesus over two thousand years ago. Because we lived in the country, Mom always told us it was easier for the Three Wise Kings to park their camels outside our house than a house in the city. We had no reason not to believe her.

We loved Three Wise Kings day because the Magi made us feel so special. No one else in our school seemed to receive a nightfall visitation from these Middle Eastern monarchs. And though legend proclaims the Three Kings brought Jesus gold, frankincense, and myrrh, we were very pleased to receive a piece of fruit, a bit of candy, and about twenty-five cents in coins from them each year.

As long as I can remember, my parents created magic in our lives. One year, Mom excused herself during dinner. While she was away from the table, we saw a camel slowly walking by the window, his hump bumping up and down. We shrieked with excitement and awe, knowing the kings had arrived!

We didn't realize Mom had purchased a huge stuffed camel and was outside moving it along past the window to keep the magic alive. The next morning, we awoke to find strands of gleaming jewelry strung everywhere on the bushes and vines around the house. To solidify the magic, we found camels' hoof marks and a good amount of camel dung beside the house! To top it all off, we found a note attached to one of the bushes. The note was an announcement that it had been a great year for the Magi, so they had decided to share their wealth with us.

I vividly remember the sensation of utter delight, when we stepped outside and spotted the shimmering jewels hanging from the trees! I will never forget it. "We're rich, we're rich!" My siblings shouted. Although we loved the fruit the Magi left us, seeing the glimmering baubles adorning our vines was magnificent. We couldn't wait to go to school to tell our teachers and our friends about these extraordinary gifts. Surely others had experienced their delights.

But no one else had.

In fact, our ingenious parents had created the illusion solely for us with used costume jewelry from Goodwill and horse manure from our barn. The nuns at school, recalling our wide-eyed awe when we retold the tale, chose to keep our parents' secret. But when we told the other children, we were met with disappointed looks. To our dismay, none of them had encountered such riches on the branches of their trees. We were so dismayed that our friends had not been favored by the Magi that we immediately shared our booty.

We were loved so devotedly by our parents and, even though we rarely received the Santa gifts that we'd asked for, had so much magic in our lives that we didn't realize we were poor. On Christmas Eve, snug under our covers, when we heard the jingling of Santa's sleigh bells and the snorting of his reindeer on our roof, we squeezed our eyelids together happily. As soon as morning dawned, we ran downstairs to the fireplace—the only heat in the house—and eyed the presents beneath the tree while we warmed up.

We always attempted to hide our disappointment at the small number of presents, but we weren't very successful. Seeing our disappointment, Dad would assure us that we had been very good children that year. Then he would add that since Santa hadn't left anything under the tree, perhaps we should take a ride around the ranch to see if Santa had dropped anything from his sleigh as he flew through.

Sure enough! Down at the barn or dangling from a grapevine would be a few special gifts for each of us. Once, a bicycle was sticking out of the chimney with a note attached that read: *Sorry, it wouldn't squeeze down.*

Today, my children delight at the magic they experience year-round in our household. The Three Wise Kings always manage to visit, leaving behind sweet juicy fruit as well as shimmering jewels or coins. And though we live on a mini-farm, through the magic my parents instilled in me we've managed to stage some pretty convincing camel visits.

> *"Take special joy in sharing the Nativity scene with friends and family, by placing it in a prominent place in your home during the holidays."*

BY NAOMI LEVINE

The Seemingly Insignificant Present

A light snow was falling on the Long Island Expressway as I drove into Manhattan the evening I moved out of my home in Bayside, Queens. To avoid late-night driving, I had rented a studio apartment near the West Side Actors Theater, where I attended classes, rehearsed, and performed most evenings. Alan, a fellow thespian, borrowed his boss's truck to transport my two sofas, table, chairs, small chest, and bookcase. Richard, Santiago, Jimmy, and Paul pitched in to help. From as far away as Omaha, Nebraska, to as close as Fair Lawn, New Jersey, the members of our repertory company meshed into a theatrical family—always ready to help one another.

A recent convert from Judaism, I invited many of these Christian and Jewish friends to celebrate Christmas Eve with me. Early arrivals, Jill, MaryAnn, and Eddie were with me at nine o'clock when there was a knock at the door. Carefully setting my crystal wineglass on top of the bookcase, between the fish tank and the Nativity crèche, I walked the few steps to the door. When I opened it, Alan entered carrying a small Christmas tree. It was a delightful and unexpected gift!

We all participated in arranging the little tree on a table near the window. Then Alan accepted my thanks and a drink, saying that he always worked part-time before the holiday selling Christmas trees, and that he could not stay long because his boss expected him to dump the unsold trees into a wooded area along the Hudson River. After a moment, Eddie suggested he save himself the trip and donate the rest of the trees to a good cause. "Just give them away," said Eddie with a smile. We all thought that was a great idea but realized it was not our decision. Alan had to do what he felt was right.

After Alan left, I located a box of ribbon and a pair of scissors. Jill and MaryAnn used them to make small bows to decorate the tree, while Eddie strummed on his guitar, and I prepared hors d'oeuvres in the kitchen nook. As other friends arrived, they joined in the fun and helped decorate the tree.

An hour later, there was another knock on the door. It was Alan again, all smiles. "I took Eddie's advice," he said. "Parked on the corner of Ninety-second Street . . . people passing by were surprised and delighted and really happy to receive free Christmas trees. Then a TV cameraman stopped and filmed us for his feature story about how New Yorkers spend Christmas Eve. It'll be on the Eleven O'clock News!"

Alan did indeed appear on the television screen that night. We cheered when we saw him waving his mittened hands in the air, barking, "Free Christmas trees! Step up and take the one you want." People grinned into the camera shouting, "Merry Christmas!" as they headed home, shouldering Christmas trees that had been rescued from the dump. Out of the corner of my eye, I watched as Alan and Eddie high-fived each other. I smiled happily. This is what Christmas is all about.

Nearby, etched in soft lamplight, stood the seemingly insignificant Christmas present Alan had given me a few hours ago. This ordinary little Christmas tree, now decorated with red-and-white bows, had set into motion an outpouring of the true Spirit of Christmas. I felt myself glow with warmth, both from the wine and from the knowledge that many families who lived near the corner of Ninety-second Street— given the same seemingly insignificant Christmas present as I had been—were, like me, looking upon their present with a similar smile on their faces. I knew their trees were also etched in light that shone from the windows in their homes. And I knew, with the surety that only Christmas magic can provide, that just like mine, their present wasn't insignificant at all. On every Christmas since, gentle reminders throughout the season bring back the memory of that special holiday when love, emanating from the heart of one, encompassed so many.

BY CHARLENE A. DERBY

Bayberry Memories

The funny thing about traditions is that it's so easy to start a new one.

That's exactly what my sisters and I did one Christmas when we returned to our rural home in southern Michigan. On break from college, we joined Debbie, our younger sister, in carrying out the family traditions we all loved. By the end of our first weekend home, we'd baked and decorated sugar cookies, boiled up a batch of fudge, and gone caroling with our friends. But that Sunday afternoon Mom dropped the bombshell.

"Cousin Wilma has offered to host the family Christmas dinner this year," she said over afternoon snacks. "She's asked me to bring vegetables and pies."

"Oh," I said, glancing at my sisters, all of whom seemed a little deflated. "We can still help, I guess." We'd been looking forward to spending Christmas morning helping Mom prepare dinner for our extended family. We cherished the chatter and clatter created by the five of us cooking together in the farmhouse kitchen. Mom usually got up at five to start the turkey and called us shortly thereafter. Breakfast was a cup of coffee and a slice of toast on the run while we baked, boiled, and stewed. This Christmas, things would be different.

"We can go shopping later this week, after you girls have finished your Christmas shopping," Mom continued. "I'll start a list."

Seated around the dining room table the following morning, wrapping gifts, Rose Mary suddenly looked up. "Let's fix a Christmas breakfast for Mom and Dad!" she exclaimed, pleased with her suggestion. "It could be a surprise. Now that we don't have to cook a big dinner to serve here tomorrow, we'd have time."

Millie pointed her scissors at Rose Mary and shook her head. "You know how hard it is to surprise Dad. We've never been able to surprise him with his birthday cake, and we try every year."

"This could be different," Debbie said, pausing as she readied a bow for the gift she'd just wrapped. "If it's in the morning, he might not guess."

I glanced into the kitchen. Mom was busy preparing soup and sandwiches for our lunch. Confident she was distracted by her duties, I whispered, "We could bake those refrigerated cinnamon rolls—the ones that come with orange glaze icing—and we could buy some real orange juice—not that powdered stuff Mom gets all the time."

"Yes," my sisters chorused, "and we could have a candlelight breakfast. Mom's got those bayberry candles the bank gave her when she cashed out her Christmas Club account. We could use those!"

The idea took off like wildfire. By the time our gifts were tucked under the tree, our plan was complete.

Later that day, Mom was surprised when all four of us offered to join her for the grocery store run. When we got to the market though, we split up. I stayed with Mom, helping her select the freshest fruits and vegetables for our contribution to Christmas dinner. Rose Mary headed for the refrigerated cases to get the rolls and juice. Millie and

Debbie disappeared into another aisle to pick up a Christmas-themed tablecloth and paper goods. While I distracted Mom, they paid for their purchases and stowed them in the car. When they rejoined us, Mom was none the wiser.

"Would you girls like me to fix anything special while you're home from college?" she asked.

We grinned and shook our heads.

Back home, I helped Mom unload the car. Millie and Debbie smuggled the paper goods upstairs, while Rose Mary buried the juice and rolls behind the milk in the spare refrigerator on the back porch. Then we slipped into our Christmas Eve routine, trying to hide our excitement.

After supper that evening, we gathered in the living room to enjoy the lights from the Christmas tree. While Dad tuned in the broadcast version of *A Christmas Carol*—one of his favorite Christmas traditions— we snacked on popcorn, hot chocolate, and apples. Around ten o'clock, we kissed our parents good night and scurried upstairs to bed.

When my alarm rang at six on Christmas morning, I silenced it as quickly as I could. Rose Mary, who shared my bedroom, was up in an instant.

"Get up *schweschder*," she said, pulling off my quilt. "I'll get Millie and Debbie. You get the paper goods."

Dressed in flannel robes and warm slippers, we crept down the dark stairs more purposeful than a pack of elves. Hoping to avoid rousing our parents, we closed the door between the kitchen and the living room. Soon the tablecloth was spread and paper plates set out. When Millie lit the bayberry candles, the spicy scent mingled with the aroma of cinnamon coming from the oven, creating a magical aura around our secret preparations. Apparently, however, we weren't quiet enough.

"*Was is letz?*" Dad asked, using a Pennsylvania Dutch phrase that meant, "What's up?"

"Dad!" we said in unison. "It's not time to get up yet! We'll call you in a few minutes."

Next, we heard a timid knock and Mom's voice. "Daddy wants to know if you girls need any help."

"We're fine, Mom, you and Dad relax," we replied, being careful to keep the door closed.

By six-thirty, our table looked like a photo from the *Good Housekeeping* magazine. The steaming rolls were nestled in the center of the table surrounded by glasses of "real" orange juice, and the candlelight gave everything a festive air. Together, we threw open the living room door and began singing (to the tune of "We Wish You a Merry Christmas") "*Won't you get up and come to breakfast, won't you get up and come to breakfast, won't you get up and come to breakfast, we won't bring it in here.*"

As Mom and Dad joined us in the warm kitchen, their faces reflected the happiness we felt.

When our quiet family breakfast was finished, Mom smiled. "That was delicious, girls," she said, as she prepared to clear the table.

"*Danki*, thanks," Dad added, setting down his coffee. "That sure was some surprise." Then he grinned. "I mean, that you girls could get up at six without being called."

"Daddy, don't tease us," I said, pretending to slug him in the arm. "We get up at college, you know. *You* taught us to take care of ourselves, after all."

Dad pulled me into a hug. "You're Daddy's girls, all right," he whispered in my ear before letting go. He turned to Mom and held out his hand. "Let's go, Dorrie. The girls can join us for gifts when they've finished up in here."

Soon the Christmas tree lights twinkled against the frosty dawn and strains of Bing Crosby's "White Christmas" drifted into the kitchen.

As my sisters and I lovingly wiped and folded our Christmas tablecloth that morning, we had no way of knowing that we'd reuse it for the next ten years—until Debbie married and moved out. Nor did we anticipate "fancy" future breakfasts with homemade scones, egg casseroles, stewed fruit, and gourmet coffee. We didn't even know that the last breakfast we'd enjoy together as part of this new tradition would include spouses for us older girls and the gift of grandchildren for our parents.

We never could surprise our folks, but after several years they came to accept the fact that *we* were in charge of breakfast. They graciously accepted our gift of hospitality and enjoyed sleeping in, until we called them with a new carol parody each year.

My parents are gone now, but as I light the bayberry candles on my Christmas centerpiece, the scent reminds me of that first breakfast my sisters and I prepared for them. The excitement of trying to surprise our parents drew us closer together, and the idea of doing something for the people who had provided us with so many rich traditions brought more joy than any gift we might have found under the tree.

"In memory of a loved one, listen to their favorite song on Christmas Day."

BY AMBER BRECHT

Angels We Have Heard on High

B ig fluffy snowflakes spiraled down, turning the evening sky into something spectacular. Ordinarily the beautiful scene would have touched my heart. Today all it did was fill me with an overwhelming sense of disappointment. Despite the thickness of my down coat, I shivered.

I was starving, and frozen, but most of all, I wanted to get this over with. John and I had been searching for wedding locations for weeks. For one reason or another, church after church had turned us down. *Would we have to drive clear through the state of New Mexico to find a church that would accept us?*

Tucking my cold fingers securely in John's hand, I let him hurry me along the narrow winding streets of Old Santa Fe toward the object of our search. "This place probably won't take us, either," I muttered irritably, breathless from trying to keep up. Without slowing down, John shrugged. "If it doesn't . . . then . . . we give up." He looked down at me. "We've done our best."

A few months earlier, I had called my father and told him we wanted to marry in a civil ceremony. "Short and quick," I announced. "No fuss, not a lot of people."

From the silence on the other end, I knew he didn't approve. Then I dropped the final bombshell. "We're thinking of flying to Vegas."

I could almost hear Dad's sharp intake of breath. "I want you to get married in a church," he said quietly. "Grandpop would have wanted it."

Those five simple words were the reason we were out in this blasted cold in the first place. If this minister said no, we had zero choice but to break my dad's heart.

My German grandfather died when I was sixteen. Of all the grandchildren, he had been closest to me. I spent many hours puttering about the garden with Gramps. I helped him pick strawberries and sell corn and tomatoes at his roadside stand. Gramps made wonderful Sunday dinners of roast "bif" and mashed potatoes. He had a magnificent tenor voice and often sang or hummed as he worked. Loving and kind, Grandpop was the glue that held our fractious family together.

After his death, the family scattered to the winds. But on the rare occasions when I spoke with my cousins, Gramps always seemed to come up in the conversation. We all wished we had thought to record Gramps as he sang "Ave Maria."

A restless spirit, I went to college in a different state and then checked out four more states in quick succession. As the busy years passed, my thoughts turned to Grandpop less and less.

Still hurrying me along, John looked down and smiled. His teeth gleamed white against his dark beard. "We're almost there," he said. "Wait till you see it."

By now the snow was falling harder, glittering in our hair like tiny stars before winking out. Here, in the old part of town, traditional *farolitos* began to illuminate the darkness. Glowing atop adobe walls and outlining paths and sidewalks, they enveloped the city in light and warmth. The wonderful smell of tamales and green chiles mingled with the falling snow and a sudden hunger pain reminded me of how ravenous I was.

Halting before a wrought-iron fence, I looked up at the beautiful old Gothic chapel—so distinct from the traditional adobe-style buildings of the rest of Santa Fe—and felt a chill cascade down my spine. The shiver was not due to the cold, but rather the scene that had appeared before me. Lovely stained-glass windows cast soft elongated shades of red, blue, and green onto the snow, causing something to tug at my heart. This place was special.

Still clutching my hand, John waited for my response. Finally, I tore my gaze away from the chapel and peered up into his hopeful face. "It's beautiful."

Within seconds, we had ducked through the carved double doors. I watched in fascination as candle flames sputtered and cast wild shadows against the walls as the chapel door swung shut behind us. The little church was enchanting. Scarlet poinsettias lined the altar railing and sculptures filled the niches. The magnificent wooden spiral staircase wrapped around itself to reach the loft. Peace and warmth filled the room. I forgot about my hunger and previous disappointments; there was no room for anything unpleasant in this place. It was too lovely.

But as tears welled up in my eyes, I realized it wasn't just the beauty and serenity of the place that had captured me. It was the music that now soared to the rafters, filling the tiny chapel.

Alarmed, John scanned my face anxiously. "What's wrong?"

I couldn't answer. I was transfixed by the gray-haired pianist bent over the piano reverently playing "Ave Maria." It was as if my grandfather were there—I could see his twinkling blue eyes and smell the Old Spice aftershave we grandkids endlessly gifted him with each Christmas. I saw the blue flannel shirt and the red suspenders he wore when he gardened. As the chords of the pianist faded, it was as if Gramps was beside me once again, singing in his rich tenor voice.

A year later, I stood in my wedding dress and veil outside the same chapel, my arm linked with my father's. A few snowflakes drifted down as we listened intently to the same gray-haired pianist. As the last strains of "Ave Maria" mingled with the snowflakes, Dad put his handkerchief away and took a deep breath. He adjusted my veil, and then cleared his throat.

"I love you, Dad," I whispered.

He smiled. "I love you, too, honey."

Though many years and many miles separate me from the place where I grew up, shivers still run down my spine when I recall my first glimpse of that chapel, and the night I heard my grandfather singing once again—as beautifully as any angel. Since then, every Christmas, I put on a CD of "Ave Maria" and once again, my grandfather's beautiful voice fills me with peace.

"Discover the holiday spirit this season in the heart of downtown. Check out the magical window displays, and drop a coin—or two—into a street vendor's hat."

BY PAT GALLANT

Piano Solo

There's an anonymity about New York City living that is accepted and, at times, even welcomed. We have privacy. We know who our neighbors are, but we don't really know them. We can be sure no one visits unannounced. Christmastime here embraces this anonymity. But ask any New Yorker—there is nothing quite like Christmas in New York. We may not provide the quiet of sitting around a country hearth with cushions of snow surrounding us, but we have hustle and bustle. The feeling in the air is electric.

The draw to go downtown to see the window displays on Fifth Avenue, along with the grand Christmas tree at Rockefeller Center, is inescapable. It holds the memories of many fine movies and—more important—the memories of people raised here, people who call this large city home. It holds *my* memories. So on this pre-Christmas evening, I venture forth with a friend, and open that photo album that is Manhattan.

As we stroll along Fifth Avenue, the energy is palpable. People scurry about, carrying armfuls of shopping bags. It's a cold night and the wind gives a firm push at our backs. Chestnuts roast on vendor's open fires, just as the song depicts. There is shoving and tugging and irritation inside stores, as tired patrons rush to buy last-minute gifts from stores open late to accommodate them. Outside, shoppers crane their necks over crowds to get a glimpse of the fantastic window displays.

As it nears 10 P.M., we're ready to call it a night. Since it's impossible to find an empty taxi, we continue walking down Fifth Avenue, among the anonymous crowds. The pushing and shoving crowd from inside the stores has now moved outside. As the wind picks up, it begins to snow and the temperature drops. Drained shoppers attempt to outmaneuver one another in their chase to secure a taxi.

From a flurry of snowflakes and wind appears a somewhat bedraggled-looking man, pushing a small weather-beaten piano on wheels. He rolls the piano up onto the sidewalk along the curb, and pulls down a folding chair from atop the piano. He deftly opens the chair and plops down. We look on, but little surprises us in Manhattan.

The man is winded but determined. He places an empty cup on top of the piano and begins to play. I watch as his bare fingers slide along the keys. I look down at my own fingers, frozen and aching from the cold, and a spark of wonder grows in my chest. *How can he play with such ease?*

The notes to "Silent Night" fill the air. A few people stop. Then more people. A man in the crowd begins singing. Then a woman. Then another person, and another. My voice and my friend's mingle with the others as strangers join hands and sway back and forth to the music. No one jumps to grab the lone empty taxi that drives by. Soon everyone is holding hands and singing. A policeman smiles and looks the other way, ignoring the fact that street peddling is illegal.

The man's cup, once empty, now runneth over. It is, after all, Christmas. A few more carols are sung. When the man finishes playing, the crowd disperses, as everyone once again begins his or her fade back into anonymity.

But in the midst of that Manhattan moment, something magical transpired. I am left feeling that, for those of us who shared this special moment, all *really is* calm, and all *really is* bright.

"Enjoy a family walk in the forest on Christmas Day. Select a special tree—your special tree from this day forward—and return to it every year with special treats for the wildlife."

BY HEIDI LEE OVERSON

A Purposeful Journey

O ur family started a beautiful Christmas tradition in 1998, while visiting my parents' farm in southwestern Wisconsin. On Christmas Day, I took my husband and our two young daughters for a walk in the woods.

We all carried apple slices in our pockets, just in case we found a nice place to sit for a snack. My girls' little legs stepped high through the deep snow, bravely trying to keep up with our bigger strides. We didn't get far—just across the small spring-fed creek and up the banks a bit—when Mari, eight, and Kristen, six, started to get tired and cold. Their noses and cheeks turning rosy, they looked longingly back toward the warm house and the promise of hot cocoa.

I sighed, realizing our winter walk was a bit too ambitious for little girls. We stopped beside a Charlie Brown fir tree and contemplated what to do. Reaching in her coat pocket, Mari pulled out her apple slices.

"Let's leave these for the animals, Mommy!"

We all agreed it would be a nice Christmas treat for the deer and squirrels. After we had placed our treats around the little tree, we went back to the house and the promised cups of hot cocoa.

I didn't think too much of that walk until the next Christmas rolled around. The year had brought us many changes—the gift of a son, Jacob; the death of my father; and the loss of my parents' home, in a fire. The farm stood silent, in transition. The woods, however, remained the same: quiet, proud, and magical in their snowy splendor. I thought of our friend, the fir tree, and decided to visit it on Christmas Day. Baby Jacob stayed home with his papa, while the girls and I trekked out into the forest. We carried several grocery bags filled with popcorn, fruit, and birdseed. Stepping across the creek, we walked toward our tree. Like the girls, it had grown.

Excited, we strung the popcorn on its waiting branches, sprinkled the surrounding snow with fruit and birdseed, and stepped back to see the wildlife's Christmas bounty. With warm hearts, we walked away, vowing to bring even more treats the following year. Crossing back over the creek, we paused and turned around. Birds were landing on the branches, pecking at the popcorn. We smiled, and Mari and Kristen giggled, thinking that the tree must feel honored to be chosen as the woods' special Christmas tree.

Every year since, the whole family has made the trek to the fir tree on Christmas Day. Every year, the tree gets bigger, just like our children. Decorating the fir tree helps remind us how much our family has changed; the group that takes the hike across the creek and through the woods is different every year.

Jacob now runs in front of our family, throwing snowballs and antagonizing his sisters along the way. And in 2004, we added another child, Hallie. While Papa has always carried her in his strong arms, this year she will walk alongside of us. Mari and Kristen, now teenagers, begrudgingly go with us, but deep down, I know they still think it's special. Sadie, our old, yellow Labrador, joined us five years ago. Once full of bounce and love of the snow, she will follow slowly this year, her arthritis and heart disease taking their toll. But despite how much we have changed, the farm is where the most change has taken place. It has seen my parents leave and my family rebuild where the old house once stood. I know it's appreciative that we didn't give up.

The woods, too, have changed, but still remain a place of wonder—soul-changing, inspirational, and filled with magic. The forest is a sheltering, sustaining place to all manner of wildlife that give us the purpose for our Christmas journey each year. The holiday feast we offer our wildlife friends is our way of honoring all living things.

That first Christmas walk, taken so long ago, gave birth to a family tradition that has provided us with a very special way of sharing the love we feel for one another and for God's creatures. Our purposeful journey both soothes and heals us, and somehow prepares us for what is yet to come. Each in his or her own right reflects on past years—their losses and gains—and with awe-filled eyes we gaze up at our beautiful fir tree and speculate on what great things God has yet in store for us.

"Having trouble getting the children off to bed on Christmas Eve? Christmas pajamas will do the trick!"

BY JO RAE JOHNSON

PJ Presents

D ing dong! The doorbell chimed on cue as it has every Christmas Eve for the past thirteen years. I watched from the couch as my children, Timothy and Lauren, raced from opposite ends of the house and collided at the door.

When the kids were little, staying up alone on Christmas Eve was difficult for a single parent of two small children. My biggest fear was that I'd nod off, while I waited on the little ones to fall asleep. Far too early and at the risk of being caught, I would begin the time-consuming process of assembling hidden gifts, while trying not to make a sound. Rarely was I successful.

One year in particular, the excitement of the holiday had been building all season. By the time December 24th arrived, it was hard for any of us to come down from our holiday highs long enough to have sugarplums dancing in our heads. Naturally, when I learned of a particular tradition that was touted to be the best cure for getting children to sleep on Christmas Eve, I was elated as well as relieved.

Around 8 P.M. on Christmas Eve, a neighbor placed two wrapped packages on our front steps. After ringing the doorbell, she ran around to the corner of our house to hide and listen for the squeals of joy as my children discovered the gifts at the door. Each year, the presents are wrapped in Christmas paper unlike any wrapping paper under our tree. And each has a note attached. In an unfamiliar handwriting, the note reads:

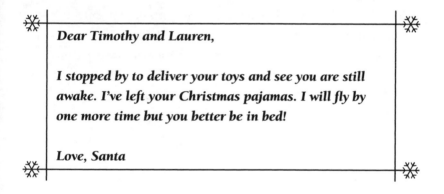

Dear Timothy and Lauren,

I stopped by to deliver your toys and see you are still awake. I've left your Christmas pajamas. I will fly by one more time but you better be in bed!

Love, Santa

In the beginning, I had to read the note to them, but all too soon, my children could read the note for themselves. The gentle reminder from Santa Claus, noting that Christmas Eve is a busy night for him, motivated my children into their new pajamas and into their beds. Before you could say reindeer paws, they were asleep!

Believing in Santa is a lot like believing in God. It takes faith. According to Kris Kringle, from the classic movie *Miracle on 34th Street*, "If you can't accept anything on faith, you are doomed to a life dominated by doubt." When children are told there is no Santa, Christmas is never the same. Pajamas that come from Santa enabled me to retain just a small part of the wide-eyed wonder that is lost when we no longer believe.

Lauren and Timothy are now fifteen and eighteen. Assuming they'd outgrown this tradition, I reluctantly suggested last year it might be time to give it up. They were very vocal in their opposition to the change. So, at least for now, Santa still visits our house. These days I've taken over for my neighbor. My biggest problem is appearing to look innocent, while catching my breath from the quick run from the front steps to the couch.

I've enjoyed this ritual almost as much as my children have. As each year passes and my teens show less enthusiasm over one more holiday activity, I face the reality that soon they'll be out of the house and on their own. I will be left clinging to the memories of my laughing little towheaded boy, and his sister, with eyes sparkling like green twinkle lights on the tree, posing for pictures in their footed Santa pajamas.

If Santa could bring *me* one gift this year, I'd ask that the holiday traditions we've shared as a family never come to an end.

"For a taste straight from heaven, spend a few hours in the kitchen creating your family's favorite recipe."

BY MARGARET LANG

Recipe from Heaven

My teenage daughter, Karin, stuck a broken cookie in her mouth, and carefully sprinkled colored sugar on the tray of cookies she had just pulled from the oven. She wrinkled her nose.

"Not as tasty as Grammy's Snowball cookies—by far," she said, reminding me again of something precious that had been lost.

"No, they aren't," I agreed. We'd sung the same forlorn tune every year since my mother's passing.

I missed Mom, especially at Christmastime, which she had ensured was filled with wonder, including her Snowball cookies—everyone's favorite culinary treat. At her festive parties, guests discovered that the round white cookies surpassed all the other brightly colored ones. Nobody could eat just one Snowball. A gathering of twenty-five people polished off fifty—easy.

During the blustery holiday winters of the past couple of years, I'd often daydreamed that the recipe would swirl down from heaven like a perfect snowflake. The vision seemed real—I could actually see the recipe fluttering downward, Mom's fine handwriting proving to me it had come straight from her hand in heaven, to my hand here on earth—but of course it wasn't. Mom was gone, and along with her had gone much of the magic of the holidays.

"Our house would look better outside with more lights, Mom," Norm, the second of my teenage children, said, interrupting my reverie, as he poked his head in through the back door and smiled.

I smiled back, as he dusted the snow from the top of his head. We watched the snow sparkle for a moment or two before disappearing into nothingness.

I moved toward the garage door. "I'll look for some."

After a thorough search, I had rounded up another couple strands. Intent on passing them to Norm, who was in charge of decorating the outside, I took a couple of steps toward the door. Out of the corner of my eye, I caught a glimpse of a dingy box beneath the huge pile of decorations we'd inherited from Mom. One sweep of my hand across the surface dust revealed the name of a mover. I frowned. The same mover who had transferred Mom's stuff to our house? *Hadn't every carton from her estate been emptied out years ago?* I laid the holiday lights aside and looked at the box. In seconds, I had torn open the flaps with trembling fingers. Inside were reams of old accounting papers—nothing interesting—which would explain why I hadn't bothered to sort them before.

The disappointment I felt was so great, tears stung the back of my eyes. Why couldn't there have been something special from my mother in this box? It made me realize how very much I missed her. As I relegated the contents back to their dismal container, my fingers brushed against something hard at the bottom. Investigating, I found a small wooden box and slowly opened the lid. It appeared to be filled with recipes—Mom's recipes! Tears sprang to my eyes, and I gasped at the wonder of finding the recipe box tucked in with our Christmas decorations. This was almost too good to be true.

The markers read: hors d'oeuvres, salads, meats, potatoes, breads, sauces, candy, desserts, and finally, at the very back—cookies. My heart pounded. Recollected smells of yesteryear bombarded my olfactory sense. I levered out the tightly stuffed cookie recipes and looked through them—card by card—then again more carefully, my mouth watering as I read the ingredients to so many loved recipes. Every one of Mom's delectable delights was there. Every one, that is, except the sought-after recipe.

"Where is it?" I wondered aloud.

Deeply disappointed, I consoled myself with memories. As a little tyke, my hands had barely reached the powdered sugar-covered Snowballs on Mom's counter. How I loved to grab one, then lick the powder off my fingers.

As I got older, I realized the secret wasn't in the powdered sugar. The secret was in Mom's light shortbread. Before Mom had time to work her way down the long row with the powdered sugar snow, I always took a plain ball—or two—from the end of the assembly line. She never scolded me for the commandeered cookies.

Mom's cookies, so much a part of herself, had made a wonderful tradition. I shivered from the chill in the cold garage. My memories were getting me nowhere. I put the recipes back in the box. Just before I closed the lid, my eye lighted on the cram-packed cards at the front; they had no labeled category. I hadn't noticed them before.

I tugged. They didn't budge. In exasperation, I yanked hard. The tattered white cards broke free and scattered out of my grasp.

I caught a few cards in midair and began reading recipes written in Mom's familiar, but now faded, script. *Hot Crab Spread, Chicken Ruby, Date Bread*, and then . . . *Snowballs*. I clutched the yellowed, oil-stained card to my chest and breathed out a long sigh. *Of course! Mom always kept her favorite recipes together at the front of the box!*

"Karin," I called as I skipped up the garage stairs into the kitchen. "Guess what? I found Grammy's Snowball cookie recipe. It fluttered into my hands just like in my wildest dream."

"No kidding," Karin said, as she took it from me. "Oh, yummy!"

Karin immediately pulled out the mixing bowl and spoons. Together, we combined all the right ingredients—even double-sifted the flour for the lightest possible shortbread. Later, when Norm peeked in the door for the long-forgotten strand of lights, the aroma drew him inside. The oven-fresh wonders were soon powdered, and three white mustaches grew, along with our satisfied enjoyment of Mom's love, sent in the form of cookies straight from heaven.

> *"Working together as a family to create a delectable ethnic dish that dates back as far as the family is one of the most perfect ways to hold on to tradition during the holidays."*

BY AL SERRADELL

The Photograph

I never would have imagined that a simple Christmas gift could put a new, more precious spin on a holiday tradition and bring my childhood memories full circle.

But it did.

The revelation occurred a few years ago on Christmas Eve. My father presented me with a legal-size manila envelope of family photographs he'd had copied. He apologized that he couldn't offer a more traditional gift, such as an expensive electronic game or a gift card to a four-star restaurant. But, knowing how much I treasured family history, he felt certain I would appreciate this present much more than any material item. And he was absolutely correct.

I immediately opened the envelope. Dozens of black-and-white photos of dear faces—many of them long since passed away—smiled back at me. I recognized aunts, uncles, and grandparents, posing next to old forgotten cars, and in the doorways of modest frame houses. There was a beautiful high school graduation picture of my recently departed mother, her gray eyes bright and sparkling before the camera, no doubt eager for the future.

At the bottom of my new stack of treasured photographs, I found a picture of three young girls. The teenagers stood laughing into the camera, their arms intertwined. Apparently the photographer had caught them in the midst of a celebration. Perhaps they'd been dancing or sharing an intimate bit of childish gossip just as the picture had been snapped. Curious, I asked my father their names.

"Don't you know?" he laughed. "You've known them your whole life."

I shook my head.

"You mean you can't recognize your grandma Lupe and her sisters?"

Shocked, I studied the photo, until finally I picked out Dad's mother in the center, to her right, Aunt Mercedes, and on her left, Aunt Maria. Having known them only as elderly women, I had never even considered them as once being young carefree girls. The trio of loving yet time-worn women, who had adopted a perpetually firm, no-nonsense manner until the day they died, had always seemed old to me.

According to my father, the picture was taken in Jalisco, Mexico, at Grandma Lupe's quinceañera, shortly before they immigrated to the United States in the 1920s. As it turned out, because the family home was raided and burned by the revolutionaries a few weeks later, this was one of the few surviving photos of Dad's mother.

For the remainder of the evening, I was unable to put the snapshot of my grandmother and her sisters out of my mind. The following day was Christmas. As our family gathered for dinner, I was reminded of a special holiday I had spent with Grandma Lupe in Los Angeles, nearly forty years ago.

It was December 1969, and my maternal grandfather was deathly sick. That was the year I learned about the Hispanic tradition of making tamales for the Christmas dinner, a tradition many in my family still honor. I was a novice, but along with my paternal cousins, I helped Grandma prepare for the feast by separating and cleaning the cornhusks that were to be filled with the meat and masa mixture. All day, we wiped down the insides of the husks and then stacked them into tidy piles that seemed to reach over my head. The cooking part of the tradition was strictly kid-free; my cousins and I were ordered to bed, so that Grandma could finish the process undeterred.

That night proved to be a restless one for me. I was awakened long before sunrise by the heavenly aroma of steaming chicken and pork tamales. I recall hearing voices, and not just Grandma's.

We had company.

Slipping out of bed, I crept past pallets of sleeping cousins and followed the delectable smells and laughing voices to the living room, which separated the kitchen from the rest of the house. I immediately recognized the familiar patter of Grandma's sisters, Maria and Mercedes, as they rattled on in a mixture of English and Spanish. The three women had completed the tamale-making process and were returning the kitchen to order.

As they worked, they talked about a Christmas they'd spent in Jalisco many years ago. It seemed they were planning to leave Jalisco because the revolutionaries had come from the mountains and stolen the livestock and their money. They recalled it hadn't been much money, but it had been all they had. The three women reminisced over the miracle. Despite that injustice, the family had somehow managed to gather all the ingredients to make tamales for the holiday meal.

I listened quietly as Aunt Maria recalled how they had thought they would not find enough to eat. Grandmother agreed and then recounted the story of how they had not only found food for tamales, their parents had also surprised them each with a pair of homemade dolls that Christmas.

My eyes were wide as I listened. *The revolutionaries stealing their food? The family on the brink of starvation?* I was shocked to realize how much suffering my family had endured. Quietly, I returned to my pallet, saddened by the knowledge I had learned. Yet, over the years, I failed to understand the full impact of that memory—until nearly forty years later, when my father gave me a photograph of three young girls.

Now, as I gaze at the picture of Grandma and Aunt Maria and Aunt Mercedes, I see three women who gathered together every Christmas Eve not to dwell on the sad events of their youth but who celebrated their survival by continuing to make the traditional feast. To them, the familiar activity of slathering meat and masa onto a cornhusk, and then steaming the tied bundle to perfection was probably more precious than sitting around the Christmas tree opening gifts purchased from a store. This was their tradition—just for them—the sharing of memories and strength. Perhaps the tradition also reminded them of a special time in their lives, before all the horrors and misery robbed them of their childhood, when they were simply three teenage girls who lived an innocent and carefree life, like any other teenage girls.

Many years later, I continue the tamale-making tradition not just to celebrate a cultural event but in honor of three resilient women whom I am honored to call "Mi familia."

"Nothing says Christmas more completely than the scent of a freshly cut pine. Join Dad in the forest and find the perfect tree for your family's holiday celebration."

BY TRISH AYERS

finding the Perfect Tree

Snow hid the view through the picture window, but the sound of the wind as it tousled the giant oak tree outside like a cornstalk during a Missouri summer storm filled my ears and left nothing to the imagination. Barely awake, I walked past the window with the blurry-eyed vision of a sleepwalker. Mom hardly glanced up from her pacing as I entered the kitchen, where Dad sat, coffee in hand. Christmas music sprang from the radio, competing with the howling wind.

It was Saturday morning and time for me to make biscuits from Grandma Berry's recipe. Dad had taught me how to make them years earlier. At the time, it had seemed an honor. I hadn't realized the honor would be accompanied by an early call from my warm bed every Saturday.

Seemingly unaware of my presence, Mom's mouth puckered as she cracked eggs into a bowl. "Arlie," she asked quietly, "do you think you should try to find Beverly?"

Dad snorted. "How? There's over a hundred acres out there."

Though I was still foggy with sleep, the concern in Mom's voice registered. I looked up at Dad. Realization dawned amid a flutter of anxiety. *Bev had gone to pick out our Christmas tree, the same as she'd done every year since we moved to the farm.* That first year there had been no money for a tree. Bev had refused to accept it. Instead, she'd wandered the woods until she'd found what she said was the perfect tree, returning hours later and convincing Dad to go back out with her. This year would be no different.

Mom's arm efficiently whipped the eggs, her eyes still trained on Dad. "She's been gone over an hour and the sky's not looking good."

Dad shrugged. "She has to find the perfect one. I sure hope she remembers our ceiling is not as tall as the sky. I swear, every year we have to trim the tree to fit in the living room."

I reached for two cups of flour to begin my morning chore. After I'd dumped the flour into the bowl, I glanced toward the window. It did look pretty rough outside, and Bev wasn't the outdoor type.

Mom poured the eggs she'd been scrambling into a skillet. "Storm's coming in. Temperature's dropping fast."

Dad sipped his coffee, his eyes never leaving the window. "Dogs will take care of her." He nodded, as if in reassurance to himself. "She's dressed warm."

I added a heaping tablespoon of baking powder and a teaspoon of salt to the flour mixture just as the wind gusted, setting the pear tree to dancing wildly. Out of the corner of my eye, I watched Mom walk toward the picture window. When her back was to me, I reached into the sugar canister, scooped out a tablespoon of sugar, and quickly dumped it into the flour mixture, stirring quickly so she wouldn't notice. Dad noticed and winked.

"Now remember to make a well from the dry ingredients to dump the liquids into," he said. "The biscuits won't taste right if you don't."

Dad smiled with pride, as I pushed the dry ingredients up around the sides of the bowl—just the way he instructed. *Forget to make a well? How could I possibly forget?* He reminded me every Saturday.

Mom walked back into the room, her mind made up. "Arlie, it's getting rough. If it gets much worse Bev won't be able to see to make it home, especially with her glasses steaming up."

Dad shook his head. "She was wearing those stupid contacts."

"It might be a good thing today," Mom mumbled as she walked to the stove and began making gravy. "If she's not back by the time I get done here, I'm going to look for her."

Concerned, I looked at Dad. I needn't have worried. He was already walking to the back porch for his outdoor clothing.

Confident Dad would find Bev, I returned to the task at hand. As I mixed the dry ingredients into the well, my mind drifted to Great-Grandma Berry. I envisioned her learning to make biscuits while cooking over a fire in front of a teepee. When I came out of my daydream, Dad was fully dressed.

"How are you going to find her?" Mom asked.

Dad kissed her on the top of her head, "Now don't you worry."

Suddenly, a whoosh of air from the back door filled the kitchen, and Bev stumbled into the house. Mom ran to her, felt her wind-burned face and stripped off her gloves. Bev's hands were almost as red as her face. Mom gently rubbed them, pulling her across the room.

"Stand by the stove," she ordered. "Your sister has it warmed up for biscuits."

I nodded proudly. "Four hundred twenty-five degrees."

Dad grinned at Bev. "Well, Sissy, did you find us our Christmas tree?"

A tear rolled down Bev's face, as she looked up at him. "I did, Dad. It was perfect. I started to walk around it to make sure it looked good on all sides, when the wind blew my contact out."

Mom gasped. Beverly was nearly blind without glasses or contacts.

"I was at the top of a hill and my contact started to roll down the hill. Everything was a blur, and I didn't want to come home missing a contact. I know how expensive they are. So, I spent over an hour looking for it with one eye closed."

"How in the world did you see?" asked Mom.

Bev shivered and moved closer to the stove. "I finally sat down in the snow and bawled my eyes out, which wasn't too smart because the tears froze to my face. Then I remembered the Bible story about praying when things get rough. I pulled the dogs around me and asked God to help me find my way out of the woods with only one eye."

Mom stopped setting the table and grabbed a tissue.

Bev turned from the stove, her eyes as wide as her smile. "I looked at the tree, so I could remember it and started walking down the hill. When I reached the bottom, something glistened. It was my contact!"

For a moment, we all stared at Bev in astonishment. *How on earth could she have found something as small as a contact in that storm?* Then a chill crept down my spine, and I sniffed back tears. Dad cleared his throat gruffly, as he, too, reached for a tissue. After a moment, he cleared his throat a second time. When he was in control of his emotions again, he put his arm around Bev. I watched as his gaze met Mom's over my sister's head. In that second, nothing mattered except our family reunited in our warm kitchen. The icing on the cake was the knowledge that not only had God been there to help Bev find her contact and her way home, he'd also helped her find another perfect Christmas tree!

> *"Make a centerpiece for your Christmas table—a gingerbread house, or your own sweet creation."*

BY SHANNON JACOBYANSKY

Tracking Twinkies

It all starts with a trip to the store, to pick out the essential items for the family centerpiece. As the first ingredient—Twinkies—which is what makes our efforts a true masterpiece, comes into view, my kids giggle, and my son Abraham picks up a box and sets it into the cart. I see the excitement on their faces and know what's on their minds. They'll all want at least one before this project is finished.

"We better get another box," I say, and they nod happily.

Next, we scurry to the baking aisle for frosting—but not just any frosting. It must be vanilla. These are instructions directly from Daddy, who single-handedly came up with this idea for our own special Christmas tradition. I put the frosting in the cart. Abraham reminds Ruth and Samuel, his younger siblings, not to eat the icing or lick the knives when we make the masterpiece. I envision the amount of frosting that will end up in tummies instead of on our masterpiece and turn around to pick up another tub of frosting.

Now it was time to find the pretzels. Not the twisted variety, says my husband's voice in my head, only skinny pretzel sticks will do. I let the children grab a bag of the required size and drop it into the cart. Ruth licks her lips and rubs her tummy in great anticipation of eating the salted treats.

I smile and touch her sweet face. "I better grab another bag." She nods happily.

Wheeling the cart around, I head toward the candy aisle. This is everyone's favorite part of the trip. This year the kids picked Life Savers, M&Ms, and gumdrops in an array of colors; some years we used colored marshmallows and peppermint candies. My own mouth starts to water as I think about M&Ms. Better get some for myself, I think, as I grab another bag.

In our dining room, we stack everything on the table, where it will remain until Daddy comes home. The kids walk by the table several times in quiet anticipation. Each will add his or her own designs to bring perfection to our treasured family tradition.

As soon as Daddy pulls into the driveway, the children rush to the door. The man of the hour is greeted with hugs of jubilation and little hands pull him toward the table. Within seconds, the tradition has begun!

First, we unwrap the Twinkies, then we open the tubs of frosting, and I break out the butter knives. Abraham retrieves individual bowls for the pretzels and candies and dumps them into the deep dishes. Meanwhile, Daddy retrieves the big tray from the bottom cupboard— the one we always use to display our centerpiece.

One by one, everything comes together, and before we know it, another magnificent Christmas Twinkie Train, complete with Life Savers wheels and a gumdrop for the engine funnel, sits proudly on our dining room table. Pretzels have become train hitches and logs for loading, and M&Ms are transformed into quarry rocks.

Our children urge me to get the camera and take a picture of this year's Christmas tradition . . . a masterpiece indeed!

My husband, Bill, originally came up with the idea of the Twinkie train. We made our first train when Samuel was two and Abraham was eight years old. Now the children are aged seven, eleven, and thirteen and still get excited when it's time to make the Twinkie train together as a family.

"Spread a little Christmas cheer this holiday season. Visit the local Giving Tree and take a tag or two. There's nothing more rewarding than purchasing a gift for someone in need."

BY AMY AMMONS MULLIS

Too Much Christmas

Shopping in the mall at Christmastime is intoxicating: Santa "ho-ho-hoing" in center court, free samples of sausages with spicy mustard sending enticing aromas into the air, and stacks of clever new electronics that flash, beep, and buzz in department store displays. Dazzled by blinking lights and blaring carols, I cruised right by it the first time. The second time, I slowed down and spotted the Christmas tree designed for the people whom Christmas had forgotten.

The decorations on the lonesome artificial tree were paper tags I'd recognize anywhere. As long as there were tags on this tree, I knew there were people in my own town who wouldn't be getting any Christmas gifts. No Christmas presents, no Christmas goodies. Chances are they were the very folks who could really use a warm winter coat and a pair of shoes for their toddler or pajamas for the baby. Traditionally, people choose one tag, but I always have trouble stopping at one.

Biting my lip, I reached for one tag. A little boy's mama wanted him to have a jacket—and a tricycle. Overcome with the possibility of helping her reach that goal, and perhaps helping someone else, too, I reached for another tag. An elderly gentleman needed a bathrobe. The longer I looked at the tree, the more it seemed as if the paper tags were multiplying before my very eyes—how could I *not* take more tags? Realizing the scope of need represented by those small tags, my eyes burned with the sting of tears and the gaily lit Christmas lights blurred together.

One of my best qualities is the wholehearted pursuit of a goal. This is a good thing when it comes to cuffing socks, losing ten pounds, or making twenty-six cupcakes decorated like ladybugs for a second-grade class party. It's not such a good idea when it comes to volunteering for a morning of duty at the school library—when I'm not sure where I'm going to find a spare morning—or deciding to entertain all the relatives for Christmas in my duplex apartment before I've counted all the spare cousins and brothers-in-law. It wasn't until I was back in the car that I stopped to count the paper tags I had taken. Five—I'd done it again, only this year money was tight. I thought of my own two boys, whose wish lists grew every time they watched cartoons and whose sizes changed every time I looked the other way. I thought of the utility bill, waiting impatiently on the kitchen counter for a check to fill the envelope. *How would I ever afford Christmas for five extra people? Yet how could I leave the tags behind?*

When I got home, I went straight to call Mom, the person who helped me through all my past challenges and adventures and who always had an encouraging word. After I'd told her what I'd done, she was silent.

"We'll talk about it next weekend when you're here," she said reassuringly. I agreed and hung up the phone.

Without delay, I spread out the tags on the kitchen table and began to scour sales circulars and tally totals. I checked the calendar and counted paydays. Suddenly, my head felt as heavy as my heart. I dropped my face into my hands. This was just too much Christmas to manage.

The road to Mom and Dad's house seemed long that weekend. Christmas carols competed with static on the radio and I sang along halfheartedly. Each mile marker that whipped past seemed to count off another reason I should be more responsible. By the time I made it to the farmhouse, I was a little girl again, ready to throw myself on the mercy of my parents.

I opened the door slowly and peeked in. Surprised at what I saw, I pushed my way into a Christmas wonderland! With a flourish, Mom put the finishing touches on the big red bow for a package covered in snowflakes and candy canes. She added the box to a teetering pile under a twinkling Christmas tree. Dad, a veteran of World War II and forty years of fatherhood, perched on the seat of a gleaming red and white tricycle, was carefully adjusting the handlebars with a wrench.

Reaching for another box and a fresh roll of wrapping paper, Mom looked up and smiled. "Hand me the tape?"

I draped my coat on the corner of the recliner, now buried under a stack of toys and boxes of chocolate Santas, and joined her on the floor.

By the time we were through, we had enough packages to fill the back of the family pickup and the trunk of my car. The memory of Dad pushing that tricycle through the mall to the gift station is a moment that will be fresh in my mind long after my eyesight grows dim. Of all the lessons I learned that year, my favorite one came from my wise and wonderful parents in a moment as bright as the star atop the tree: there can never be too much Christmas!

"Set a meager dollar limit on gift giving this year, and then add one more gift, the priceless gift of sentimentality—the only gift that can be fully given from the heart."

BY BARBARA FARLAND

Trash to Treasure

After a full three months of marriage, our house was still in shambles. Many an unopened box was left to be tackled in the spare room. Our front porch was always piled high for the Goodwill pickup. And then there was me, the nagging wife, who constantly harangued her husband to clean it up, ship it out, scrap it—scrap it all!

Like many new brides, I was determined to build the best of nests for us. In turn, I fell victim to a terrible case of compulsive decluttering—you could call it "The Great Purge"—and its ugly symptoms surfaced every weekend, every evening, and during every dinner conversation. In pursuit of the best-run and best-regarded of homes, there was nothing outside my eyesight, earshot, and arm's reach that wouldn't be considered for the trash heap.

As the Christmas season approached, my ailment lingered. Though other women were daydreaming about what they'd receive in gifts, I almost dreaded the thought. Not only would it throw a wrench into my purging plans, but it would also threaten yet another of my wifely obsessions: penny-pinching.

Try convincing your husband of a holiday without presents. It's not easy. I finally agreed we could exchange gifts, but with ground rules firmly attached. We volleyed on the dollar limit, with me starting at twenty.

"Twenty-five," countered my husband, Terry.

I shook my head. "Twenty-two-fifty and not a cent more," I replied. "And," I said with eyebrows raised, "remember to keep your receipts."

"Okay, deal," he agreed.

Weeks went by, decorations went up, and a bedecked and bejeweled Christmas tree stood prominently in our living room. Eventually, all forty-five dollars' worth of purchases were stacked underneath it, the tree skirt hardly visible. As I gazed upon our spread, I was proud of my resourcefulness and confident that I had my husband beat. I tucked my receipts in a safe place, certain—100 percent certain—that Terry would pummel me with awe-inspired questions about how I managed such a feat.

The day finally arrived to divulge where our budgets had taken us. It was Christmas Eve, and I allowed my husband to dig in first. As predicted, he was amazed by all his loot.

"Wow, a sweater . . ." he gushed, as he opened one box and reached for another. "Cool, I wanted this—how did you know?" I smiled happily and puffed up with pride. I had duly impressed him with all that I had accomplished.

Then it was my turn. Before me was a tall tower of gifts, proof that my husband had also done well. I opened package after package, revealing numerous items from my wish list. When I reached the bottom of the pile, I did my calculations. He had clearly reached his dollar limit . . . but then one more gift appeared. He's in for it later, I thought. And with reluctance, I tore in.

My breath stopped, my jaw dropped, and my eyes filled with tears.

The gift before me had been made by my father when he was just a teenager. Nestled inside the wrapping paper on my lap was a rather crude rectangular pine box Dad had used for storing tools. When he eventually found the funds to invest in a *real* tool chest, the box had been discarded, buried under a mountain of equipment in a shed on his parents' homestead. Fifty years later, when my uncle died, and the farm was put up for sale, the box was rediscovered. Still in one piece but layered in half a century of grease and grime, the box was put on the auction block with other leftovers. Someone might want it, they'd reasoned.

That someone had been me.

Fresh out of college, I had no money to put toward the classic artwork, antique furniture, and other more desirable items up for bid. A confessed sucker for sentiment, I kept my eyes peeled for some kind of meaningful, reasonably priced piece of memorabilia. When Dad shared the story behind the junk on display, my hand immediately shot up to signal the auctioneer. That dirty old box was mine for two dollars.

Grease and grime? Hardly! It was more like the world's most impenetrable tar. Don't ask how many times I soaked that thing in Dawn dish soap, scoured it with my best steel brush, or tried to make use of it somehow, some way, despite its stubborn coating. A few years later, the box was delivered to my new home. But despite my original affections, even that precious box was no match for The Great Purge. Along with a bunch of other trash, the box was gone forever. Or so I thought.

Without my knowing, Terry had rescued it from the trash bin, took it back to the garage, and tucked it away for just the right opportunity. He devoted every moment that I was away, or distracted, to restoring the long-lost golden luster to what would become a cherished heirloom.

Every Christmas since, in addition to sticking to our originally set dollar limit, there is another catch. We must present each other with something priceless. The priceless gift can be a scarf made from scrap yarn or a spice holder made from portions of Plexiglas. All that matters is that these gifts are expressions of the treasure both of us hold most dear: time spent *for* and *with* each other.

I learned quite a lesson that first Christmas. Sure, I take care of our home, but now it's for an altogether different reason. These days it's not so much about proving my skills as a good wife, as it is about *being* a good wife to Terry, my best friend, my husband.

> *"Make Christmas morning even more special by baking something delicious for your neighbors."*

BY ANNE MCCRADY

The Taste of Christmas

S ome Christmas traditions are carefully handed down from one generation to the next. Others develop gradually, usually because of something we did that ends up blessing us in some powerful way. Our family's favorite Christmas tradition is one of the latter.

Some years ago, when my husband and I moved, we were totally overwhelmed and exhausted by his new medical practice, stacks of boxes to unpack, and keeping up with three small children. We both wanted to be the kind of parents who created wonderful family memories, but with so many commitments it seemed impossible.

Luckily, dozens of retirees, all ready to lend a hand, lived nearby. Our next-door neighbors on one side welcomed our middle son for backyard gardening and an occasional trip to town. The neighbors on the other side kept their kitchen door open for cookies and punch. One man, who lived down the street, loved when the children helped him with jigsaw puzzles. Another precious couple made each of our children birthday cakes. Around the corner, Mrs. Hooper, a widow who sat near us at church, loved having company.

One year, a few days before Christmas, on a night when my husband was able to get off work from the hospital to be with us, I decided to repay the many favors our neighbors had done for us. I bundled the children in their warmest clothes and took out my guitar. Together, we walked the neighborhood, ringing doorbells and singing carols to the wonderful people who had become our adopted grandparents.

Everyone was so glad to see us! Some invited us in. Others gave us candy canes or hot chocolate. It was so much fun that we decided to do the same every year.

One holiday evening, as we finished our night of caroling at Mrs. Hooper's house, she opened her door and handed us a metal pie pan wrapped in foil. An envelope was taped to the top of the frozen contents.

"Merry Christmas!" Mrs. Hooper said, smiling. "You're so busy, and my own children have always loved these."

As soon as we got home, we read the note:

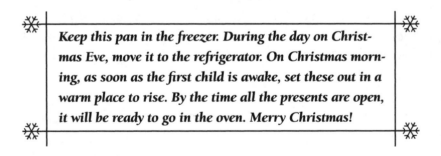

Keep this pan in the freezer. During the day on Christmas Eve, move it to the refrigerator. On Christmas morning, as soon as the first child is awake, set these out in a warm place to rise. By the time all the presents are open, it will be ready to go in the oven. Merry Christmas!

My children immediately lifted the foil and peeked inside. It was full of frozen homemade cinnamon rolls! Not only did I not have time to bake, I didn't know the first thing about how to make homemade cinnamon rolls. It was a perfect gift.

A few days later, as we wrapped presents on Christmas Eve, I took the foil pan out of the freezer as directed. At our Christmas Eve church service that evening, we sat with Mrs. Hooper and her family. My children excitedly told Mrs. Hooper they couldn't wait to eat the cinnamon rolls the next morning.

That night, when I put the kids into bed to listen for Santa's sleigh, they reminded me not to forget about our special breakfast. I promised I wouldn't, but by the time my husband and I had finished putting toys together and setting gifts under the tree, I was exhausted. I fell into bed, forgetting to set the alarm.

The next thing I knew, light was streaming in the windows and three small children were jumping up and down beside our bed.

"Get up!" they shouted. "Santa came! It's time to take out the rolls!"

As they scrambled into the den to see what was under the tree, I quickly set the cinnamon rolls on top of the dryer and turned it on. In the den, we all took turns opening packages and showing everyone our gifts. When everything was cleaned up, we remembered the rolls. Everyone ran to check.

"Wow!" two-year-old Patrick shouted.

"It's magic!" His big brother Andy added. "Look how big they are!"

With the heat of the dryer, the rolls had puffed up inside the pan. Once in the oven, the magic continued, filling the kitchen with the delicious warmth of butter and cinnamon.

At our Christmas table that morning, still exhausted, I was grateful to Mrs. Hooper. As we bit into the delicious rolls, now dubbed *Mrs. Hooper Cinnamon Rolls*, I looked around the table at the precious sugary faces, and tears came to my eyes. I had never known either of my grandmothers, but I was sure this must be one of the best parts of having a grandmother.

As soon as breakfast was over, we called Mrs. Hooper to thank her and to let the children tell her about their other Christmas gifts. She was delighted.

For the next decade, well in advance of Christmas Eve, Mrs. Hooper called us to pick up our pan of Christmas cinnamon rolls. And without fail, we called her on Christmas Day to thank her for her breakfast rolls and to share our holiday with her.

Then one year, my husband, who also doubled as the physician for many of our adopted grandparents, told us that baking had become too much for Mrs. Hooper.

"I don't think she's up to making our cinnamon rolls this year," he said quietly.

My children, college students by then, were heartbroken. Mrs. Hooper's rolls and the Christmas morning phone call had become a very important part of our family's holiday routine. The following year, my daughter, Kate, home from school for the holidays, took up the challenge.

"We will just have to learn to make cinnamon rolls ourselves," she explained.

And so we did, though my kitchen ended up completely dusted with flour by the many less-than-appetizing batches we tried in our efforts to get them "just like Mrs. Hooper's." Even the men in our family got into the act, rolling out the dough and devising an extra-sweet mixture to spread inside the spirals. Best of all, it was something fun we could do together.

These days, we have many Christmas traditions we love: caroling, church services, story-themed trees, gingerbread houses, and toys for grownup kids. Still, our favorite tradition is spending one day each December in the kitchen, mixing and kneading and rolling, and one hour each Christmas morning at the breakfast table together, telling stories and delighting in the remembered taste of friendship.

The best part of this memory is that a good deed came full circle. Once we had learned how to make the cinnamon rolls, we returned the blessing and delivered delicious *Mrs. Hooper Cinnamon Rolls* to Mrs. Hooper herself.

"Save a few pennies this Christmas season and wrap your gifts with newspaper."

BY CARLENE RAE DATER

The Funnies

When I close my eyes, I can see the room as clearly as if it were yesterday, the scrawny pine slumped in front of the window, the bent tips of its leaves already dry and beginning to yellow. Some of the colored light bulbs had burned out, while others winked in random patterns. The bright silver tinsel was creased and twisted from numerous years of use, but in the eyes of two little girls, it was the most beautiful tree we had ever seen.

The Christmas my family remembers most vividly took place when I was five and my big sister, Cherie, was four years older. Mother stood in the kitchen, wrapping all the relative's gifts to take along to the big family celebration on Christmas Day, while my sister and I helped Dad finish decorating the tree with stings of popcorn.

When Mom stepped into the living she had such a long face, we knew something was terribly wrong. She looked at Dad, stricken. "I've run out of wrapping paper. What are we going to do?"

Nothing was open in Minneapolis, Minnesota, on Christmas Eve—not a drug store, not a Kmart, not even the corner grocery store. We still had all our own precious family gifts to wrap and no holiday paper left. It was nothing short of a tragedy.

"Well," Mom said, trying to make the most of a bad situation, "we'll simply have to put our presents under the tree without wrappings."

My sister and I turned toward our father—the only person who could possibly solve this awful dilemma. Daddy paced around our small living room, scratching his head, with a solemn look on his face. Cherie and I held our breath, waiting. We knew he was deep in thought. Daddy took another lap around the parlor, and suddenly, a wonderful smile lit up his face.

"I think I've got the answer," he said, as he walked with purpose toward the kitchen. "Follow me."

We hurried behind our father as his long legs carried him thorough the kitchen and down into the dark, dusty cellar. In the corner, we spied the huge rack of old newspaper we'd been collecting for the school paper drive.

With hands on his hips, Daddy nodded once. "Perfect. Help me pull out all the sections of the papers with cartoons. They'll be ideal for our holiday wrappings."

Laughing and giggling, Cherie and I yanked out a big bunch of funny papers and hauled them upstairs. Then each member of the family grabbed a stack of newsprint along with some tape, tags, and loops of ribbon, and scurried off to different parts of the house to beautify our individual treasures.

There wasn't much money in those days, so the gifts weren't fancy. Cherie and I usually made something for each of our parents in school. We also pooled our allowance and bought a box of handkerchiefs for our father. Daddy had terrible hay fever, so he always appreciated our gift.

"Hurry up and finish, girls," Mom called. "We have to get to bed so Santa can visit."

At the sound of our mother's voice, we completed our unique bundles and hastened to place them lovingly under the tree. The four of us stood in front of that tree and decided this year's gifts were surely inside the prettiest packages we'd ever seen.

The addition of the funnies, to our Christmas celebration, made everything seem even more magical. We quickly got on with our Christmas Eve ritual: cookies, milk, and one chocolate-covered cherry for Santa. We brushed our teeth, threw on our nightgowns, said our prayers, and jumped into bed, knowing full well that we would never be able to sleep that night. But sleep we did, and soon it was morning—Christmas morning!

We raced to our parents' bedroom and bounced on their bed to wake them. That task accomplished, we hurried into the living room to make sure Santa had been there. Yes, there was the proof! *More* presents were nestled beneath the tree, wrapped in funny papers, the glass of milk was half-empty and one cookie had a big bite taken out of it. Mom explained that Santa thought wrapping gifts in funnies was a great idea, so he had done it, too! Cherie and I felt so honored that Santa had liked our family's idea that we squeezed each other happily.

We distributed the gifts from under the tree and then took turns opening them one by one. What fun we had ripping and tearing as we unwrapped our gifts. For the first time ever, we didn't have to be careful and save paper!

Soon, the floor around us was littered with new clothes, a few toys, and a big pile of ripped, torn newspapers. As I stuffed wads of paper into the trash, I recall thinking that this was one of the best Christmases I'd ever had. I still think so.

The Christmas we ran out of wrapping paper started a whole new family tradition. The next year, when Cherie and I went with Mother to start our Christmas shopping, we all decided it would be fun to use cartoon funnies for family gifts again, instead of wrapping paper. Every Christmas since, Cherie and I vied to find the most colorful, brightest, weirdest cartoons we could lay our hands on all year long. We hid our treasured Christmas wrap, only pulling the paper out in December, just in time for Christmas. We delighted in adding sparkles, wildly colored ribbons, and faux flowers. One year, I used bandages with stars on them instead of tape. Daddy laughed until tears ran down his face.

Over the years, my sister and I have tried to keep the tradition alive. Our children and grandchildren will never really understand a world without television, computers, and a store on every corner, but they know how much fun it is to use newspaper cartoons instead of wrapping paper.

Dad's been gone now for thirty-five years, and mother is ninety-six. Every year, I make sure to wrap at least one of her presents in funny papers. When she opens that gift, the smile on her face lets me know that I'm not the only one who remembers the best Christmas we ever had.

BY JOYCE STARK

Christmas Diaries

Like most people in Scotland in the 1940s, we did not have a lot of money and could not afford lavish Christmas meals or expensive Christmas presents.

I was an only child, but my uncle and aunt and my cousins—Jacki, Andrew, and Neil—lived upstairs from us. The highlight of our Christmas day every year was a big parcel that arrived via airmail from our relatives in Germany. My grandmother on my mum's side was German. Although she had moved to Scotland when she was in her teens, Mum still had aunts, uncles, and cousins in Berlin and Hanover, who got together every year and sent us a parcel.

Similarly, Mum and Aunt Paula managed to save and get together a parcel to send back to them. Based on the items in the package we received, our German relatives were much better off than we were. But our package was just as exciting for them to open, because it contained things they could not get in Germany in the years after World War II—like coffee and sweet milk chocolate.

Our parcels from them were magical. They knew our parents couldn't afford to buy us many presents, so they always included wonderful toys such as German musical boxes, jointed wooden dolls, and mechanical animals that threw pennies into the air and caught them again in little containers around their necks!

At first, when we opened the box, we would only see white mounds of fluffy cotton wool. Half the fun was searching through the wool for packages with our names on them! The presents for our parents were separate in the big box—Mum and Aunt Paula always received a huge fresh salami. It would be hung in the kitchen carefully and turned from time to time to keep the fat from gathering all at one end. There would also be long sticks of marzipan for the adults, wrapped in dark chocolate, which we children thought tasted like tobacco.

But regardless of all the food and toys our relatives sent, the most important item in the parcel was the Christmas Diary. Each year both families would put a diary in the parcel just before it was sent. Throughout the year, our relatives in Germany wrote in this dairy, just as we wrote in ours. In the diary, we shared everyday events as well as special moments.

After Christmas dinner, we quickly cleaned up the kitchen and settled down in front of the old coal fire. Mum and Aunt Paula took turns reading from the Christmas Diary. Collectively, an anxious expression crossed our faces as we heard tales of Sophia in Hanover and her first days at her new school. The anxious expressions were exchanged for huge grins, when Mum read how Sophia and her brother, Heinz, went skating with all their friends and Heinz bumped into a girl on purpose because he had a crush on her. From Berlin, Paul and Anna wrote about how the jeweler's shop they owned near Templehauf station was getting very busy. We laughed at some of the odd inscriptions people asked for on their pocket watches and wished we could be there to see it for ourselves. We sat enthralled as our distant aunts, uncles, and cousins spun tales of holiday bliss filled with sleigh rides and great food. We nodded excitedly as they thanked us for the things we had put in our diary.

Though separated by thousands of miles, we grew up with our German cousins—bit by bit. We shared their studies, their hobbies, and, later, their romances. There were moments of great happiness and times of sudden sadness, and all were written down to be shared over laughter and tears. Without benefit of telephones, faxes, and e-mails, we still learned the easy things about their lives that could be written down, and we also learned the things that are harder to explain in writing—emotional words that painted a vivid picture of each and every relative. We learned through their words, and they through ours, how we each felt about everything around us.

Sadly, as we grew up and some of our older relatives passed away, it became too difficult to keep the diaries going. Busy lives and modern technology took over, until one January evening when the phone rang.

I had no idea my cousin, Jacki, who had married and sailed to Australia to make a life with her new husband and three children would be thinking of the same things I had been thinking about. Hearing Jacki's voice lifted my spirits tremendously.

"I was telling the kids all about our old Christmas Diaries from Germany," she said, after we had visited for a few minutes. "They had this brilliant idea to start them up again by sending you guys in Scotland their diary every Christmas—if you will do the same—just like in the old days."

I was so keen on the idea that tears immediately sprang to my eyes. From then on, the Christmas Diaries in our family became a wonderful obsession Now, this Christmas, as we sit cozy and warm with snow falling gently outside, my husband, Eric, reads aloud. It seems in Australia last year they had a barbecue on the beach for Christmas Day!

While the rest of my family listens intently, my mind drifts back to those wonderful days of our German Christmas Diaries, when the magical stories of sleigh rides mesmerized me. Sometimes, I am so deep into my memories that I can smell the salami and taste the marzipan. When those times come calling, I sigh in contentment for I know those wonderful memories are the real gift of Christmas.

"Create special ornaments that neither can be purchased at a store nor found on another family's Christmas tree, and lovingly share them with your expanding family."

BY SALLY CLARK

Christmas Shells

In the winter of 1943, when America was two years into World War II, my parents were eighteen months into their fifty-eight-year marriage. Daddy was in the Army Air Corps, stationed at an air base in Santa Ana, California, teaching chemical warfare to men preparing to ship overseas. Housing was tight, but people with beach cottages were renting them out to local service personnel. My parents were lucky enough to find a garage apartment on Balboa Island, right on the beach.

Daddy loved the beach. He loved to fish and to prowl the beach for shells. Black-and-white pictures in Mom's photo album show a young soldier in uniform, squatting in the sand with his fishing pole, studying the waves. One day, Daddy returned from the beach and announced he had been digging clams with Humphrey Bogart. Seems Mr. Bogart had a cottage on the island and a taste for clams, also. They didn't talk much, just dug in productive spots, sharing a peaceful morning of blue skies and chattering gulls.

When the Christmas season arrived, Daddy had an idea. One afternoon, he gathered buckets of scallops and lugged them up the stairs to their apartment. Mom popped them into pots of boiling water for a few minutes and soon served a tasty scallop dinner on their green Formica-topped dinette.

After dinner, Daddy cleaned and separated the scallop shells. With great patience for detail, he painted each shell in shades of gold, silver, red, and green. While they were still wet, he sprinkled them with glitter. When the paint was dry, he carefully punched a hole in the top of each one and threaded each with a small wire. Voilà! Christmas ornaments for my parents' first Christmas tree. Daddy created more than 100 shell ornaments that first Christmas, more than enough for their tree. Year after year, the shells were the first ornaments Mom hung on our Christmas tree. I grew up thinking everybody decorated with colored seashells.

When my husband and I married in 1970, Dad cut down a cedar tree for us, and Grandmother sent us her old glass ornaments and a set of large colored lights. Mom gave me some shells, just a dozen or so, but enough to carry on the tradition. Many years later, as our children married and established their own families, Mom passed on a dozen or so shells to each of them for their Christmas trees. Through the years, some of my shells have gotten broken and the paint is chipping away on the remaining few.

"There won't be enough shells in decent shape to pass on to any of our grandchildren," I lamented to my husband as we took down our Christmas decorations a few years ago.

In 1999, my parents moved into a retirement village in the large city where they had lived for forty-seven years. That year they decided not to put up a tree. Instead, Mom bought a silk Christmas wreath, covered it with shells and hung it on their front door. Neighbors commented, and questioned, and the story of my parents' Christmas shells spread.

Two years later, Daddy died.

This year, Mom moved 500 miles away from the city she and Dad had called home for fifty-five years, to the small town where my husband and I live. The move was not easy. At eighty-six, Mom is still very mobile and independent. Assisted living is difficult for her to adjust to, but she doesn't want to live alone, and she doesn't want to move in with us. Living in only one large room has forced her to give away, throw away, or sell most of her possessions.

When she decorated for Christmas this year, Mom hung the shell wreath on her hallway door. A week later, I drove her to my granddaughter's Christmas program. I was surprised to see the necklace she was wearing. It was a beautiful gold-painted shell strung on a gold chain, hanging delicately over her heart. She patted the shell gently.

"He's right here, still with me," she said, and I knew she meant Daddy.

A few days later, while cleaning through one of Mom's Christmas boxes, I found a small checkbook-size box of shells, each one carefully painted and glittered, with a tiny hole in the top. Mom was thrilled that I wanted the shells. There were enough for my grandchildren and maybe even their children. I locked the box of shells in my home safe, along with other irreplaceable possessions and important papers, and felt rich.

My dad's hand-painted shells, created in a time of war, now symbolize a time of peace in our family. The Christmas shells my parents so treasured will continue to be a treasured part of what has become a family tradition.

"Hang stockings by the

chimney with care . . ."

BY NADJA MERI BERNITT

The Red Velvet Stocking

New marriages are not the giddy happy-ever-after scenarios you find at the end of most fictional books. They're the beginning of long, complicated commitments. Second marriages are even trickier. Both partners carry memories of their first marriages—open wounds—and sometimes, worse, the fond remembrances of the good times that will never be again.

In 1983, I married a man who, like me, had been divorced. We both had kids. We both had emotional baggage. We both longed for a new life and a chance to do things right. As if that wasn't enough pressure, it was two weeks before Christmas, and I'd just moved into his house.

I wanted it to be *our* home. I wanted to feel like a bride setting up house and putting *my* touch on *our* home. But traces of his ex-wife hung on—her curtains, her dishes, her choice of blue paint in the foyer. I thanked God for the holidays and a quick fix. I draped garlands of pine boughs—festooned with maroon bows and white plastic holly berries—from an upscale floral shop, on the stair railings and across the doorways. I bought hurricane candleholders and pine-scented candles. I made sure the ornaments on the seven-foot tree were mine, mixed with two-dozen new ones we'd picked out together. And finally, the mouth-watering aroma coming from the kitchen bore the signature of my grandmother Mary: her famous apple-walnut cake.

Assuming I had covered all bases, I greeted my husband at the door after work. His delighted expression as he surveyed my handiwork was priceless.

"It's never looked this great. Seriously," he said.

Maybe he was just pretending for my sake, or perhaps he just wanted to please me. I didn't know and tried with all my heart to step beyond my insecurity and not care which it was, but it was hard. I tried to convince myself all that mattered was our celebrating our first Christmas as man and wife.

He made Manhattans, and we carried them down to the den. He started a fire in the fireplace and then joined me on the sofa. We sipped our drinks, watched the flames, and basked in the warmth of us. After a bit, he sat forward, placing his hands on his knees as if in deep contemplation.

"You know what we need?" he asked as he looked around the room. "We need stockings for the mantel."

I smiled, pleased he wanted to get into the Christmas spirit, too. "I'll pick some up tomorrow," I said. "Something in maroon and gold. I was thinking of doing the walls in a dusty sage and—"

"No sense in doing that," he interrupted. "The kids would shoot me. I've got stockings down in the basement—those hokey ones with the embroidered names. I've had mine since I was ten." He rolled his eyes in thought. "I'm sure we've got extras for you and Franny."

Extras? Did he think my daughter and I wanted hand-me-down stockings? Did he think I wanted to sort through his Ghost of Christmases Past? As my heart sank to my stomach, I took several deep breaths to regain my slipping composure.

"Come on, it's no trouble," he said holding his hand out to me. "Put your drink down and let's have a look."

As he led me down the basement stairs, I prayed this didn't ruin our Christmas. His face shone with childish expectation, as we uncovered a stack of dusty cardboard boxes. From the looks of the boxes, they hadn't been touched in years, probably since his divorce. He culled one box from the stack and sliced through a strip of masking tape.

He smiled. "These are the stockings. Go hang 'em on the mantel." He kissed my cheek. "It's a tradition."

Tradition? It struck me hard then that this was his house and his tradition. I was still a wife in name only. It would take years and years before I had a Christmas history with him and his children, or became part of their family tradition. I felt lost and out of place, and no amount of pine boughs could disguise it.

I was sure that onerous, dirty cardboard box held his ex-wife's stocking. No doubt all the happy holidays they'd shared would fly out the moment the box was opened. Not knowing what else to do, I took the box from him and trudged back upstairs.

Setting the box on the floor, I stared at it for a full minute. Finally, I screwed up my courage and parted the lid.

The stockings were there just as he'd said. The first one was made of deep red velvet. But when I read the name on the fuzzy while cuff, my heart jolted.

"It can't be," I whispered.

"Ah, but it is," he said softly. I spun around to see Bob framed in the doorjamb, his hands proudly folded across his chest. "Fooled you, didn't I?" I nodded, tears glistening in my eyes.

Bob had indeed fooled me. And as I picked up the red velvet stocking with *my* name scrolled across it in bold script, I knew my place in his home and in his heart, and I've never doubted it since.

"Prepare and share a special meal on Christmas Eve. No matter how much you enjoy the meal, you'll find you enjoy one another's company even more."

BY DOROTHY L. BUSSEMER

Oyster Stew with Mother

My mother's family was English on both sides, all the way back to the time of Queen Elizabeth I when one of my great-great-great-great-grandfathers sailed with Sir Francis Drake to meet the famous Spanish Armada. He then sailed with Sir Francis on his historic trip around the world on The Golden Hind. As a child studying history in school, I asked Mother if he had also gone pirating. Mother gave me a hard look.

"Don't be funny about your English ancestors," she said firmly.

I should have expected as much. Her own mother had been born in France to English parents serving in the British Navy. They were later assigned to Canada, where her mother grew up and met my grandfather, who, at the age of fourteen, had been serving as a cabin boy aboard a British ship and was dropped off at Halifax when he become ill. A Canadian couple took him in and reared him, and when he married my grandmother they moved to the United States, ending up in Zanesville, Ohio.

Their life here was vastly different than life in England. They made their living in Ohio, distributing farm produce and fruit from a stand in the City Market House and from a truck driven door to door by my grandfather. Because my red-haired grandmother and my tall, dark-haired grandfather thoroughly charmed their customers with their English accents and manners, they did all right.

Neither became naturalized citizens, so when it was time for her babies to be born, Grandmother always returned home to Canada to ensure her children weren't born "Yankees," or U.S. citizens. When it came time to deliver her tenth child—my mother—Grandfather's failing health kept Grandmother close to home. Alas, my mother was the only one in her family who was born in the United States.

But being a "Yankee" didn't discourage Mother from following certain traditions. She often told me stories about her parents, which included English customs and unusual ideas. Though the stories were interesting, little about my grandparents' customs made much of an impact on me except for one: eating oyster stew on Christmas Eve. Mother was proud of that meal. She told me often enough that times had been hard for her family, so hard they sometimes didn't have presents. But even when there was no money for presents, they always managed to enjoy oyster stew on Christmas Eve.

I grew up in a home based on English ideals, for Mother had inherited both her mother's beauty and many of her habits. Father was the adventuresome type, who worked in construction in many parts of the country, but he always tried to be home on Christmas Eve. He said he didn't want to miss hearing me complain about those oysters, which I detested. I used to try to coax my mother into letting me out of eating that stew, but she would threaten a migraine if I refused to eat. Because of that stew, I grew up detesting anything English.

That changed the day I was given a cat named Ragbag who would eat anything—even oysters.

On Christmas Eve, Ragbag sat on the floor beneath the table. I slipped oysters down to her while maintaining proper manners and appearing to eat my stew like a good girl. Mother was so proud of the way I was growing up and learning to love oysters! This went on for two happy years. On the third year, disaster struck. Ragbag yowled because I wasn't feeding her oysters fast enough. Mother demanded a full confession and I obliged. Though Mother looked heartbroken by the truth, she never made me eat oysters again. She continued to make the stew—but only for herself. I had a bologna sandwich and Ragbag got cat food. It didn't hurt my conscience in the least, and I liked bologna sandwiches.

I lost Mother in 1965, and the thing I miss most is watching her eat oyster stew on Christmas Eve. A week or so ago, I bought a pint of oysters and made myself a bowl of oyster stew. This time, I swirled the stew around my mouth and really tasted it. I remembered the complete enjoyment on my mother's face each time she ate oyster stew, and I suddenly understood what she had been feeling. It was good—*really good.* I smiled as I imagined Mother up in heaven clapping her hands in joy and shouting to the nearest angel, "I knew she would like it if she ever really tried it!"

These days, I make my own batch of oyster stew on Christmas Eve. As I'm preparing the stew, the years drop away until I'm back in my youth and Mother sits at the same table with me. I see Mother's happy face as she begins to eat. This time I don't rely on Ragbag to help me out. No, indeed. Instead, I enjoy the oyster stew as much as Mother does.

"Start a family tradition of your own. Take the entire family to Christmas Eve Mass."

BY BILL PEARSALL

A Family Tradition

Growing up, it didn't seem to me that my family had many traditions. Church on Christmas Eve was the exception. We never missed church on Christmas Eve. When we were young, there was no extended family nearby, so it was just my parents, me, and my younger brother. Naturally, as children, my brother and I protested when we had to leave behind a perfectly good day of play, clean up, and put on our Sunday best so we could go to church. The worse part was being forced to sit quietly for an hour! Our protests then were in vain, and this year—the year Dad turned eighty-three—was not much different.

As usual, my brother and I, and our families, had gathered at my parents' house on Christmas Eve, and once again, my brother and I were debating whether or not to attend Christmas Mass. Dad's health had been declining in recent years and he'd just been diagnosed with Lewy body dementia, a form of Alzheimers, and given less than a year to live. With a family that had grown to include two daughters-in-law, six grandchildren, and two great-grandchildren, we felt the added commotion would not help his condition, and church may not be the place for us this year.

Because Lewy body dementia falls in between Alzheimer's and Parkinson's in terms of symptoms, Dad suffered from a great deal of trouble with motor skills as well as some confusion. Just the same, this year as always, Dad settled the church debate easily.

"Mom and I are going to church and everyone is welcome to join us," he said as he stood, so Mom could help him with his coat.

A few minutes later, the entire family was on the road that led to the church my parents had attended for over forty years.

It was the same church I had grown up in, and I was awash in memories. I gazed at Dad. *Were his thoughts in the past as well?* More than any other time of the year, Christmas was Dad's time to embrace life. He was from a generation that did not talk much. He did his duty—he took care of his family—and never asked or expected much out of life. But Christmas was different. He loved the feelings of hope, goodwill, and joy that surrounded our lives, and he had made sure my brother and I were infected with the same sense of excitement.

We grew up in the days of elaborate Christmas window displays in the stores downtown. Almost immediately after Thanksgiving, Dad packed the whole family into the Chevy and headed downtown to see the lights. On Christmas Eve, Dad would speculate with great seriousness as to where Santa was, and how soon he would be in our town. My brother and I were so excited we could hardly sleep! Rising well before dawn, we'd race into the living room to see what treasures Santa Claus had brought. Over the years, Dad had given us a sense of Christmas that was much larger than any present we could possibly receive. Christmas was his happiest time of year, a time to think of mankind as a family, and that same feeling had been instilled in us.

Before the service began, I looked down the pew to where Dad sat beside Mom. She had her arm around him—not like the old days when he had to sit between my brother and me to keep us from talking or poking each other throughout Mass. He was relaxed and kept his eyes glued to his family in the pew before them. His grandchildren talked and laughed and, at any given time, at least one of the youngsters was under the pew. A pacifier had already been torpedoed into the row in front of us.

Our family was large and loud, so unlike the days of my own childhood. *Was Dad proud of the family he had made?* So many questions entered my head—things we had never talked about. *Did he know this was his last Christmas with all of us?* Though the disease made speech difficult for him, I was rewarded as I spied on him that Christmas Eve evening. The beginnings of a smile touched his face when yet another grandchild disappeared beneath the pew in front of him, only to poke his or her head out near his feet. As I watched, I realized the truth for what it was. *Christmas was magic for Dad.* It always had been and still was. Swallowing the lump in my throat, I accepted the inevitable. Dad knew his time was short, yet he was at peace.

When the service started and everyone settled down, I concentrated on the Mass, letting thoughts of Dad slip away. When the first hymn began, however, a surprise feeling of peace descended on me, too. Dad could never sing, but that did not stop him from participating. And as I watched my parents as they indulged in this most precious of activities, I knew what had caused the wondrous feeling. Mom held the hymnal, and this time Dad had his arm around her. He was not quite straight, but his head was held high and there was a smile on his face.

Actions really do speak louder than words, and I took a great deal of comfort from watching the two of them.

Dad and I never did get to speak of all the great things I wanted to talk about. But that's okay. Whenever I'm stricken with a need to know if Dad loved me or was happy, I only have to remember his actions, for he *showed* me the answer to my question, time and time again.

BY CAPPY HALL REARICK

A Celluloid Christmas

I love sappy, sentimental Christmas movies. When Clarence grants Jimmy Stewart's wish in *It's a Wonderful Life*, and Jimmy gets goofy and scares Donna Reed into the middle of next week, I'm just as frightened as she. And, for the life of me, I can't understand why those big galoots in Macy's couldn't see for themselves that Edmund Gwynne wasn't just playing a role in *Miracle on 34th Street*—he really was Kris Kringle.

There is another movie I have always loved, even though it's not considered by most people to be a true Christmas film. *Mayerling*, the romantic portrayal of a royal love affair gone tragically awry, is one of my favorites to watch during the holidays. I was reminded of it the year I went to Austria for Christmas, hoping for a snowfall, something we Southerners know little about. Arriving in Vienna, five days before Christmas, there was not a drop of snow but it was cold. I bundled up each day to walk around the city and do touristy things, like buying gifts for family that would wind up as garage sale items. I also adored the performances of

Swan Lake and *The Nutcracker,* and afterward sashayed across Philharmoniker Strasse to the Hotel Sacher for a reviving cup of hot Viennese coffee and a decadent Sacher-torte.

In short, the days and nights leading up to Christmas Day were pleasantly full, but there was one snag. I had nothing planned for the Eve of Christmas or for Christmas Day itself. Austrian merchants and hoteliers go home at midday to be with their families, leaving skeleton crews to take care of people like me.

So, that is why on Christmas Eve, I was all by myself in the near-empty hotel lobby leafing through travel brochures. Then what to my wandering eyes should appear, but a Christmas Eve pamphlet promoting a traditional Christmas Eve dinner at a restaurant in the Vienna Woods! The trip would culminate at midnight, with Mass at Mayerling.

"Mayerling," I sighed breathlessly, as I showed the brochure to the only hotel employee around. "Omar Sharif and Catherine Deneuve were in the movie. So romantic, so tragic and so...."

The hotel person raised his eyebrows and sniffed. "*Bitte?*"

I nodded vigorously, shoving the brochure under his nose.

"Mayerling," I said loudly. "*Ja?*"

Smiling, and in perfect English, he told me there were two seats left on the bus that would take us to Mayerling. Could I be ready by four o'clock?

Grinning wildly, I shouted, "Mayerling. *Ja! Ja!*"

The bus was warm and noisy and loaded with many nationalities. It may just as well have been a NATO Summit. We chugged, finally arriving at a quaint restaurant steeped in Old World charm that looked like Heidi (Shirley Temple) had decorated it herself. After a traditional Austrian Christmas Eve dinner of fried carp, roast goose, baked celery root, and marzipan, we boarded the old bus again and rode to the bottom of a hill located in the thick of the Vienna Woods.

It was close to midnight when our tour guide doled out lighted "torches" to us with instructions to walk single-file up the hill to the chapel where Mass would be said. The penitential convent, she added, had once been the site of the hunting lodge where Crown Prince Rudolf (played by Omar Sharif) and his mistress, Baroness Mary Vetsera (played by Catherine Deneuve) sealed their fate in a murder/suicide pact.

"The altar," she said to her captive audience, "stands over the very spot where the bodies were discovered in the prince's bedroom." A chorus of expected "oohs" and "aahhs" followed.

I had hiked almost to the top of the hill, when I felt the first snowflake. I turned to look behind me, and what I saw took away what was left of my breath. Dozens of flickering hand-held torches twisted, turned, and meandered up the hill, illuminating an otherwise black night. The only sounds I heard were soft footstep crunches on the icy ground that accompanied the gentle purr of falling snow. Well-known movie director C. B. DeMille, whose keen eye and flamboyance permeated movies in the twentieth century, could not have staged it better.

At that moment, all romantic illusions of Rudolf and Mary, and their tragic love affair, left my conscious mind. Gone were my visions of Omar and Catherine, no longer there to cloud my vision of such a sacred moment. The quiet midnight torches below were etching themselves on my soul, as though they were indestructible strips of celluloid.

Eat your heart out, C. B.

I have seen unforgettable images in my lifetime, but none as indelible as the one stamped on my soul that Christmas Eve. I still cherish the vision of that quiet group of people, ambling up a hill at midnight to honor the Christ Child, born to bring us love, peace, and hope for a better world.

I expect one day I'll take that special journey again. Till then, I will stroll the main streets of St. Simons Island on the blackest of holiday nights. I will look at blinking electric lights in the store windows and be reminded of the flaming torches that once twisted and turned, on a snow-covered hill, in faraway Austria. And I will never forget that special midnight at Mayerling.

"On Christmas Eve, the most special evening of the year, let the magic flow through you. After the younger children have gone to bed, try your hand at being Santa's helper."

BY ANN HITE

𝕭𝖊𝖑𝖎𝖊𝖛𝖎𝖓𝖌 𝖎𝖓 𝕸𝖆𝖌𝖎𝖈

In December 1969, Dad was in Vietnam, and the rest of our family had moved to Atlanta to be closer to my mother's side of the family. We had an apartment that was too small to hold my brother, me, and Mom. We solved the problem the way most military families did: we made do. The days were cold but lacked the snow I loved so dearly. Instead of a white holiday, ours began with a cold hard rain that clung to the tall pine trees like an icy coat. It matched my mood. When Dad had left, nearly a year ago, a giant chip had come to rest on my shoulders; nothing Mom did pleased me. As far as I was concerned, Christmas was just a silly bunch of emotions for little kids like my five-year-old brother, Jeff.

Three days before Christmas Eve, Mom lugged in a box. I watched from the short hallway that separated the living room from our two cramped bedrooms.

Jeff was immediately alert. "What's in it, Mama?"

"It's a tree." Mom said, looking at me pleadingly.

"A tree?" I rolled my eyes.

"Come on, Ann," she said, as she opened a box and pulled out a green metal pole. "Let's give this a chance. We have all the old decorations. It'll be almost the same."

"No way, Mom," I replied and turned to walk out of the room.

"Help us, Sister," Jeff begged. His little voice made me angry. Jeff was so young. He sometimes had a hard time remembering Dad. But I wanted no part of a Christmas without my father. When we were shipped back home from Germany, and Dad left for his tour, I promised I wouldn't change. I'd freeze time until he returned.

Besides, this tree was the stupidest excuse for a Christmas tree I'd ever seen. I refused to put one ornament on limbs that looked like bottle cleaner bristles. At least it wasn't a tin-foil tree, like my grandmother had sitting in her big picture window, with a color wheel light, reflecting off the silver branches. That was too tacky for words.

On Christmas Eve, Mom insisted on eating dinner with her family at my grandmother's house. "She's cooking a big hen and a roast," Mom explained.

Hen and roast, what was Mom thinking? "What about turkey and ham? We always have turkey for Christmas."

"We're going, Ann," she added, not waiting for my response. "This is a new tradition for our family." The hurt hung in the air, building a wall between us.

"We can't be a family tonight," I snapped, stomping off to my room to hide the tears.

Mom followed. "Ann, we owe it to your little brother to have a good Christmas. Your dad would be disappointed."

I sobbed into my pillow. "It's not fair to have Christmas without him. You're just forgetting him. You don't even care."

Mom folded her arms across her chest. "Really, is that what you think I'm doing?" She stepped closer. "I'm trying to give Jeff a good

Christmas. He's five and still believes in the magic of the night. Next year, he might not." She looked at me hard. "*I* still believe in the magic."

"I'm too old for Santa," I spat.

"That's too bad," she replied. "Because when you think you're too old for Santa, life becomes dull. Now get ready and try to have a good time tonight."

Later that night, after Jeff was asleep in the twin bed across the room from mine, and I lay on my back staring at the ceiling, thoughts of Dad filled my head. I saw him in his old chair, watching me as I flung wrapping paper around the room. How I wished I could be five again. Then I thought of how Jeff looked when he told my uncles and aunts that Santa would be coming to our apartment that night. Once upon a time, I couldn't sleep waiting for Santa to come, either. But I'd outgrown all the lies.

As I lay there feeling empty inside, the most horrible bumping and trembling vibration got my attention. I listened hard. The sound came again. This time there was a rhythm: *bump, bump, bump.*

When I was little, Dad and Mom always told me to listen for the sound of reindeer on the roof, and what the pawing and scraping would sound like. I glanced at Jeff just as the sound came again.

Butterfly wings stirred in my stomach. A clinking sound came with the next bump. I eased out of bed, tiptoeing like a child.

Mom's bedroom door was closed. The sound came from the back of the apartment. I could feel the vibration on the bottom of my feet. When I looked out the window, the only thing I saw was the cold moisture built up on the glass. I eased the backdoor open. This time the whole balcony and staircase to our second-story apartment shook. My breath caught in my chest. *What in the world was going on?* I tiptoed to the edge of the balcony and peeked over.

There was Mom, struggling with the handlebars of a brand-new bike. She sniffled as she worked.

"Mom," I whispered down to her.

She jumped and looked up at me. "Oh! Thank goodness. I thought you were Jeff." She looked at the bike. "Your dad . . . ." Her words trailed off and I knew she was crying.

In that moment, I had a crystal-clear thought. Maybe, just maybe, Mom missed Dad not being here for Christmas. Maybe she *was* just being strong.

I walked down the stairs.

"Ann, you're going to be sick. You don't have on shoes." She wiped at her eyes.

"Don't worry, Santa," I said softly. "I'll pull on the handlebars and you push."

That Christmas Eve I helped Mom play Santa. We moved in silence, setting out toys, books, and new clothes, even a gift to both of us from Dad. When I went to bed, I fell into a deep peaceful sleep.

There are moments in our lives that mark a shift from child to adult. It took a tiny apartment, the absence of my father, and the unselfish caring love of my mother to teach me my first lesson in humility and compassion, and to make me understand that giving from the heart is the most precious gift of all.

"Get into the spirit of Christmas—take turns holding the family celebration at each other's house. When the family grows too large for your house, rent a hall!"

BY J. M. PANTATELLO

ꙮaux ꙮanta

"Santa, your nose is falling off!" Six-year old Joey whispered to the man in the Santa Claus suit. As Santa adjusted the glowing sphere on his nose, Joey slid silently off his lap, clutching the Hess fire truck Santa had just given him to his chest.

Joey tiptoed toward me, tossing sly glances over his shoulder as his younger sister sat on Santa's lap. When he reached me, he waved me closer, so he could whisper in my ear.

"Daddy, I think Uncle Albert is wearing Santa's clothes," Joey said, his eyes wide. Then he pointed to Santa. "Look at his broken nose."

What could I say? I was not prepared for this. I told Al the nose was a bad idea. What was I supposed to tell Joey? Was he to learn the truth about the Santa myth at the tender age of six? In my mind, I ran through several scenarios. I looked at Joey. *Nah, this kid ain't no fool; he won't buy plan one, two, or three. The truth? Okay, what is the truth?*

I tried to remember how old I was when I learned the truth about Santa. Nothing came to mind. I looked around for my wife. As a childcare professional, she would have the right answer, or at least know how to handle this for our own children. Unfortunately, she was MIA. The job fell to me.

Joey glanced toward Santa, gazed up at me, checked Santa again, and then looked back at me. He was waiting for the truth.

A week or so before Christmas, our families gather for the traditional Christmas party. Over the years, this event has grown to incorporate fourteen families (parents, their grown children, their children, and friends). Each family sponsors the event, in turn. When they're in charge, it's that family's responsibility to raise the funds, rent the hall, and send the invitations.

Of course, with all the small children, Santa Claus has to make a spectacular appearance with presents for everyone. It was a job that fell to the volunteer who had enough courage and stamina, for it took hours to dole out gifts for each member of the family. Uncle Albert had taken on the role so often he'd even purchased his own custom-made suit. Everyone knew who Santa was, of course, except for the small children.

This year, it was our turn to host the activities, and as always, we had tons of help. Even the weather cooperated. Snow was predicted for the evening. But as I watched Joey, on his sixth encounter with Santa, a.k.a. Uncle Albert, I could see I had troubles.

Joey watched his cousins, one by one, as they scurried off Santa's lap, flopped to the floor, and tore into the colorful wrappings on their gifts. The grownups would have their turn sitting on Santa's lap last. Santa would ask embarrassing questions of the adults and teenagers, and soon everyone would be roaring with laughter. Al was always such a ham.

I noticed Joey shift from one foot to the other, as if he were weighing a great decision. He shrugged his shoulders and looked up at me, raising his eyebrows, biting on his lower lip. I could tell by Joey's expression that he was getting ready to spill the beans.

Before Joey could rat out Santa, I waved him over. Together, we strolled to the kitchen. Could Joey handle the truth at such a tender age? Even his eight-year-old sister still believed.

I hoisted him onto the kitchen table, and we stared into each other's eyes. Finally, he'd had enough.

"It's Uncle Albert—not Santa."

"And why do you think that is?" I asked.

Joey looked past me into the other room, where Santa was still shelling out gifts. He looked back at me and shrugged.

"Because Santa Claus is very busy," I said. "He has to be in a thousand other homes before bedtime, and he's running late."

Joey checked Santa again.

"Santa called Uncle Albert this morning and asked if he'd please help him out today," I added.

Joey's mouth formed a big circle. "Oh," he said slowly.

I was beginning to feel proud of myself—that seemed to go well.

Joey looked at Uncle Albert again and then back at me. His expression hadn't changed. "Uncle Albert helped out last Christmas too, huh."

All I could do was nod.

"When your family gets together this holiday season, share an uninterrupted moment together and dance like there is no tomorrow."

BY DAVID C. NITZ

The Christmas Dance

I met Amy when we were both just twelve. Seven years later, we were married.

Amy's family was a large and happy one. I spent my first Thanksgiving with this unique fun-loving crowd in the small east Tennessee town of Cleveland. It was there, a six-hour drive from their home in Salem, Virginia, that Amy's two older sisters were attending Lee College. We arrived, bringing the entire Thanksgiving feast. Despite the cramped quarters of the efficiency hotel we rented, the food was wonderful. While we ate, Amy's father slipped from his chair. Everyone pretended not to notice, when he pushed the play button on an old cassette player.

The tape started with the sound of faint sleigh bells that grew louder as the music started. Then, as if on cue, the entire room erupted into dance. I soon learned it was their traditional Christmas dance. I'd never seen anything like it.

There's no particular uniform movement to this dance. It's a free-style celebration. The kind of dance you might do if you'd just found out you had won a million dollars. Everyone danced—with no holding back—until the song ended. It was wonderful! Then, out of breath, we fell back into our chairs and laughed. Not a fake courtesy laugh. We laughed until our bellies hurt. It felt so good.

It was the same scene every year, and always the same song—Burt Kaempfert's version of "Sleigh Ride," starting with the ringing of the bells. From that moment until New Year's Day, Christmas music would be played continuously.

Since that first Thanksgiving in Tennessee, I've participated in many Christmas dances. There've been dances in Atlanta, Tampa, Wilmington, Alexandria, Savannah, more in Cleveland, and even one as far away as Louisiana. These many years later, I'm now a minister with a family of my own. I have three wonderful sons, all of whom have learned to dance *the* dance. The family is now spread out, but fortunately, we've been able to get together and dance the Christmas dance, even when we didn't feel like dancing.

Thanksgiving 1993 was cold, rainy, and dreary. The weather seemed to mirror what was in our hearts as we all hurried to an Atlanta hospital, where Amy's brother Matt battled for his life. Cancer had robbed him of his hair and more than half of his weight. It had not, however, taken any of his joy.

Folks often unfairly expect a minister's son to fit a certain mold, and Matt didn't often fit into this mold. In fact, Matt really didn't fit into anybody's mold. This handsome young man loved the unexpected. He was a people person through and through. Matt made the people around him better. He was the kind of man who made people laugh. Being a youth minister was a perfect fit for him because he found a way to use humor to share the joy of Christ with his followers. He loved people, and they loved him. This was evidenced by the walls of his hospital room, which were plastered with cards, balloons, pictures, and many unique get-well messages. It was also evidenced by the steady stream of people who came and went. The irony is that a visit with Matt was one that was sure to leave *you* better.

That holiday the entire family gathered at Matt's house. After the meal, we packed up everything and went to the hospital. When we arrived, it was obvious Matt was in pain but happy we had come. The months of chemo and his ever-weakening health were taking their toll.

At the signal, the bells began ringing, and it happened again, as it did every year on this day—everyone began to dance. Matt grinned from ear to ear. I always made sure I got some footage of the dance and of Matt dancing, because his dance routine was sure to be hilarious. There was just no telling what he was going to do next. This day was no exception. Although he couldn't get up he managed to sing, wave his arms, move his feet, whistle, offer a Matt-patented *yee-haw*, and make us laugh with his usual antics. He made faces and did absolutely crazy things, until we were all either laughing or crying. That day we did both. As the music was coming to an end, Matt looked straight into my camera and waved. It was his good-bye wave.

At the age of thirty-three, less than a month after our last Christmas dance, Matt left us for his heavenly home. His loss propelled us into shock. We tried to carry on with Christmas celebrations but were only going through the motions.

The following year, we tried to hold the official Christmas tradition, but the dance lacked its usual energy. Christmas and grief don't mix well.

Giving—that's what makes Christmas special. That's what this entire season is about. We give things away. We release them, even when we wish we could hold on to them a little longer. As I thought about it, I realized Matt's going away had made our hearts heavy but had brightened up the halls of Heaven; just as the angels had celebrated the birth of Jesus, none celebrated his death. It was a lesson we needed to follow.

The Christmas Story does not end in a manger, nor does it end with a cross. It ends with life. Jesus lives! That's the real cause for the celebration and we should celebrate every day. It seems to me that kind of a celebration calls for a dance. The kind of dance King David must have danced when the glory of God returned to Jerusalem. The kind of kick-up-your-heels dance that should be done when we realize that death does not win.

I learned from Matt that we should live our lives, knowing each day could be our last. Like Matt, we should listen for the bells, and then, we should dance.

"Begin your own particular form of Christmas tree decoration this year. Bedazzle your tree with a beadwork bonanza, or go for a change-up and cover your tree with the simplicity of elegance in the form of Styrofoam snowballs."

BY STEPHEN D. ROGERS

And Having a Ball

Twunk! That sound resonates in my mind when I think about my family Christmas, which was always filled with Styrofoam balls.

In the '70s, my siblings and I always spent a joyful afternoon making decorations, while Dad assembled the tree and strung the lights. Mom kept us in the kitchen, and out of his way, by setting out bowls filled with colored beads and glittery things, which we arranged in patterns and pinned to colored Styrofoam balls to hang on the completed tree.

I can't imagine how difficult it must have been to manage five children, as they reached over and under one another's arms for a red bead or another straight pin, but perhaps that's why Mom sang carols until we were done.

Twunk!

I'm not sure which was better, making new creations, or opening the boxes to find the ones we'd made in previous years.

Because we never labeled our work, we often disagreed on who had produced each stunningly magnificent display of sparkle, always passing off our earliest efforts as something obviously done by the youngest.

Twunk!

This annual Christmas tradition served us well throughout our childhood. Some years Mom put out bits of ribbons. Other years the pins were longer, allowing us to stack on more beads. Still other years she did away with the pins altogether and we held the beads in place with rivers of glue.

The glue treat was not repeated often.

Twunk!

I don't know where Mom got the original idea. But it was the '70s, a craftier age than the present. Perhaps families all across America were gathered around their kitchen tables making similar pieces of Christmas art. Or maybe Mom came up with the idea on her own, inspired by the desperate need to keep us from interfering with the project in the living room.

The tree never went together easily. Perhaps the reason Mom sang those carols was to keep us from hearing Dad's frustration, filling our ears with sounds a bit more festive. Thanks to Styrofoam balls and thousands of colored beads, not once did we wander into the living room to ask Dad if he was almost done. Instead, he always came into the kitchen to announce his eventual success.

Twunk!

Traditions not only provide us with some of our fondest memories, they also give us direction in deciding how to structure our adult lives. After my wife and I had a child, how could I not introduce the idea of pinning beads to colored Styrofoam balls, a craft I was sure our toddler could handle? Here was something we could all do together to usher in the Christmas season, and create an annual tradition of our own.

Twunk!

My daughter glanced at the pile of pins, grouped some beads by color, and then grabbed several balls, dropping one whenever she tried to pick up a third. Finally, she managed to grasp three at once. Her smile could have powered every Christmas light in the neighborhood.

"Balls!" she cried delightedly.

From the very beginning, she had loved balls of any size, shape, or color. While other children might be calmed with a doll or stuffed animal, she relaxed only when a ball was placed in her hands.

Twunk!

"Yes," I smiled, "we're making decorations for the Christmas tree."

I didn't need to tell her the target twice.

Off she toddled into the living room and the Christmas tree, bare except for the lights I'd already strung. She stopped in front of the tree, laid the balls on the ground, and then picked up one before straightening again.

The wind-up.

The pitch.

Twunk!

After beaming at us, she picked up another Styrofoam ball and sent it flying.

Twunk!

My wife went for the camera as the third ball flew through the air.

Twunk!

My daughter was three for three, each of the balls managing to stay in the branches. Off she went to grab another handful. By the time she'd worked her way through all the boxes, we had a dense concentration of white about a third of the way up the tree. When the occasional ball fell or bounced off, she merely grabbed it and made another throw.

She didn't decorate a single Styrofoam ball that day—nor in the years since—but she did take one of my prized family Christmas traditions and made it her own.

Over the years, she's let up some on her consuming desire to group her pitches, and now spreads the balls a little more evenly around the tree. She also throws from farther and farther back, leading me to wish we'd marked her throw lines, the way we marked her changing height on the kitchen doorjamb.

When we ask if she still enjoys decorating the tree, she always smiles and says, "I'm having a ball!"

*"No matter where you celebrate
Christmas, or what your circumstances
are when the holiday rolls around,
all it takes is one favorite Christmas
tradition to make everything feel right."*

BY PATTI MATTISON LIVINGSTON

Feast Day in Pharaoh Land

The rise-and-fall chant of midday prayer wailed from the spire of the small mosque I was passing, echoing a thousand-fold across the city. I shifted my bag of groceries from one hip to the other and plodded on down the street to our apartment. Climbing slowly to our sixth-floor walkup, I tried to shake the enveloping fog of melancholy that had been growing all day. Tomorrow was Christmas, and for the first time in our lives, my husband, Doc, and I would be separated from our family during the holiday—separated by language, tradition, religion, culture, and a distance of half the world.

As I reached the sixth-floor landing, I tried to recapture the gladness of Spirit I had felt yesterday. Doc and I had finally moved from the hotel, where we had waited several months for our apartment to be readied. In the developing country of Egypt—where I often thought time had stumbled to a stop a few centuries after the pharaohs—the lame-turtle pace of accomplishment had been a constant frustration.

Our landlady, Amina, patient and amused with our impatience, would say, "*Malish* (it doesn't matter). You move tomorrow, *insha'allah* (God willing)."

Tomorrow had finally arrived yesterday.

Amina was an attractive bustling woman in her forties, a career woman in blazer and tall heels. As a girl in her farming village, she had fought to go to school, succeeded in becoming a teacher, and now was a director in the Ministry of Education. Enthusiastically, she swept into my new life, restoring my optimism as she took me shopping for furniture and brought workmen into the apartment to build window screens and make other requested changes. She was a devout Muslim, who twice traveled to Saudi Arabia to make the grueling pilgrimage to Mecca. From her I learned—fascinated—about Egyptian attitudes, traditions, feast days, and kindness.

Yesterday, she had come up the stairs into the midst of our moving chaos. Handing me a cloth-wrapped pan containing a casserole, she said, "Wel-come. This first dinner for new home. Just make it warm a little."

Now, as I unlocked the door, I realized I had been completely preoccupied for weeks with the move-in and learning to live in Egypt. I had hardly considered the approaching holiday—there was little in Cairo to remind me. But when I awoke that morning in my Egyptian home, I suddenly remembered the date. A dense cloud of homesickness settled over me.

Today was Christmas Eve.

In September 1980, Doc and I had arrived in Cairo with a group of agricultural consultants and their families. This team of men had signed two-year contracts to launch a U.S. State Department project designed to help Egyptian small land owners—*fellaheen*—improve their farming methods and raise their standard of living. Before departure, our group had received intensive orientation in all things

Egyptian: history, religion, superstitions, and sanitizing vegetables. Surfeited with information, and euphoric with good intentions, we flew off to make a difference.

Nothing, however, had prepared me for the Cairo airport. I seemed to have fallen into a frenetic otherworld, where frenzied people shouted in strange tongues, bumping into one another—and me—amid odors of sweat and rancid cooking oil. Passing a café, I saw a cat leap onto a table, snatch something from a woman's plate, and dart away. The woman yelled, smacked the table, and continued eating.

Reality orientation had begun.

Shepherded into taxis by an expediter from the Egyptian bank that was hosting the project, our dazed group was driven across the city to our hotel. The stupefying bombardment of my senses continued. Boxlike buildings bordered streets filled with automobiles, hand carts, bicycles, buses, donkeys, and pedestrians, all undulating in pulsing streams like a flooded anthill, occasionally heaving apart enough to reveal painted white lines serving absolutely no purpose.

Because tourist season had begun, all luxury hotels were full, so we had been booked into a second-rate establishment in a scruffy area. Here, weary and befuddled, we endured air conditioners that leaked on our beds, a single elevator that broke down every day, food that often made us sick, and daily lessons in the perplexing Arabic language.

Nevertheless, as day followed day, the overwhelming friendliness of Egyptians began to reassure us. Hospitality, we discovered, was a way of life for Cairenes. The protective numbness enveloping my emotions began to slough away, slowly replaced by my recovering sense of humor and a growing affection for our cordial hosts.

Finding an apartment, where we could rest from the clamor and foreignness of the city, was our top priority. An official from the host bank introduced Doc and me to Amina. She showed us her flat—new, light-filled, and free of lingering evidences of former tenants—located in one of Cairo's better neighborhoods. Today, unlocking the door to that flat, I remembered the jubilation I had felt when we signed the lease.

Standing in the living room, other memories engulfed me. *Christmas.* I picked up a framed photograph, a recent one of our four grown children. Sinking into a chair, I stared into each young face, whispering each name. When I closed my eyes, I saw them gathered around a Christmas tree, always the center of our yuletide celebrations. A tree laden with ornaments collected over the years: World War II plastic balls. Paper chains created by small fingers. Exotic glass baubles. During the day, our children would be joined by aunts, uncles, and cousins. Piles of packages would accumulate beneath the tree. And finally, amid drifts of wrappings, the secrets of their contents would burst forth, delighting children, grownups, dogs, and cats all bonded in the warmth of family sharing.

A tap on the door landed me back in Egypt with a thump. Opening the door, I found Aziz, our building's *boab* (doorman) clutching a heavy potted plant. Dressed in a floor-length brown cotton robe, panting from the climb, he stepped inside and set the pot on the floor. His leathery face was crinkled in a smile.

The plant was a vigorous specimen of a genus thriving in Cairo. I looked from him to the pot and back, puzzled.

Reading the question in my face, he said, "Madame Amina," pointing to a paper tied to a limb. Chuckling, he shuffled out and down the stairs.

"*Shukran,*" (Thank you) I called after him. Plucking the paper off, I read: *Hapi feast day Missus Pati.*

A present!

Surprised, touched, I examined the little plant more closely. I discovered, draped across one branch, fifteen inches of slightly tattered silver tinsel garland.

A Christmas tree!

Hugging myself, I closed my eyes for a moment, imagining again the elegant fir tree I knew would dominate our children's day. A warm tide flooded through me, as I gazed again at Amina's gift, a broad-leafed little *Ficus elastica*. A rubber tree, bearing a scrap of tinsel.

A rush of exhilaration swept me. I couldn't wait to tell the kids that in Pharaoh Land we also would gather around a tree—a small but beautiful rubber Christmas tree!

"Spread some joy this season. Join the church carolers as they go door to door serenading neighbors and loved ones on Christmas Eve."

BY DIANE BULLER

𝔖taying 𝔍ome with 𝔖carlatina

Nineteen-sixty was the year my mother made me the most amazing red dress with white polka dots, white collar, and oversized bow on the back. It was perfect for a seven-year-old girl. Unfortunately, I didn't get to wear my brand-new dress to the Christmas Eve service. I didn't even get to go, despite the fact that I'd memorized my poem to recite at our little church in central Illinois farm country. No dress. No poem. Not even a bag of fruit, candy, and nuts. And, worst of all, no Christmas caroling after the program.

The doctor called it scarlatina.

I had no choice but to stay home with my mother.

I watched dejectedly as Dad ushered my two older brothers to church, while I lounged on our sofa and gazed at the Christmas tree lights. This was our second tree this year. The first one had already been stripped of decorations and replaced with a fresher version with all the original trimmings, because the next day my cousins would come for dinner. This year, it was our turn to host

Dad's side of the family of more than two dozen aunts, uncles, and cousins, and Grandma. I could hear Mom's mixer in the kitchen, grinding the cranberries for the relish and chopping the dates for my favorite dessert. I hadn't eaten much these last few days, but I would eat date cake on Christmas no matter what! Mom didn't seem to mind having to stay home. She had plenty to do before tomorrow. As I shifted on the couch, she shifted from one recipe to the next.

Would I have to stay upstairs in my bedroom the next day? Would I get to open my gifts the next morning before everyone started arriving around noon? I didn't dare ask for fear of what the answer would be. *What if dinner was canceled? Or worse yet, Christmas!*

Rather than think about the unknown, I focused on what I knew for sure. I knew I was missing hearing the other kids' poems that they had memorized—and the songs. A lump rose in my throat. How I missed the songs! I could hear Christmas carols on the old radio in the kitchen, but they only reminded me of the songs I could be singing in church and caroling. Even at the age of seven, I knew all the verses to "It Came upon a Midnight Clear."

"Are they going caroling?" I asked Mom, half hoping my family wouldn't be going, and at the same time hoping they did go so *they* didn't miss out on all the fun, too.

"I don't think so," Mom murmured, as she mixed up another concoction.

Not going? My eyes misted over. *Was I ruining Christmas Eve for everyone?* For me to miss the program was hard enough, but for my whole family to miss the caroling afterward as well! The church caroling was an event *not* to be missed. Families drove to the homes of elderly, who didn't get out on bitter cold winter nights, even on Christmas Eve. And always to a family of seven, whose father was paralyzed from polio. Caravanning from one farmhouse to another, we always waited until the whole group arrived, then we snuck up to the door to sing three or four songs. After singing, we ran back to heated cars and headed to the next farmhouse, but not before a bag of hardtack or homemade cookies was passed through the door just as we ended with "We Wish You a Merry Christmas."

As the evening waned on, my thoughts shifted from what I was missing to attempting to stay awake until my family came home. Just as my eyes were beginning to droop, Mother walked into the living room and flipped on the switch to the porch light. At that very second, I heard the first strains of "Joy to the World" coming from our front porch! I instantly sat up from the couch and pulled back the white shirred curtain. I looked out in amazement.

"Why are they *here*?" I asked.

Mom smiled. "They've come to sing to you."

I knelt on the couch, my face pressed to the frosted living room window, mesmerized by my own private choir. As soon as the songs were finished, Mom handed them the treat she had been busy making in the kitchen, and they raced back to their cars. Within seconds, Dad and my two brothers walked through the back door with the usual bag of fruits, nuts, and candy.

I have never been able to remember what gifts I unwrapped the next morning, but there are some things about that Christmas that I will never forget, including spending time with my family and enjoying a piece of delicious date cake with whipped cream. My most vivid memory still has the ability to put a smile on my face. I recall sitting at the top of the stairs—my perfect red dress with white dots and white collar, with the oversized bow in the back spread all around me—memorizing every little detail about the night before, when the church carolers had stood on our porch and sung Christmas carols just for me.

"Hold an annual house decorating in the same manner as an old-fashioned house raising was conducted! Offer a hand to someone in need, and all will be blessed by the final product."

BY CAROL NYMAN

Honoring the Son

It was my first Christmas as a widow. I was living in a new home, in a new neighborhood, and in a different state. Truly, because of all the changes, it was a different life.

I didn't have one friend in the neighborhood.

The move had been exciting but bittersweet. As the holidays approached, I pictured decorating the outside of the house for the first time—something I had never done without my husband. The decorations were sitting in a corner in the garage, waiting for the perfect day. I hated ladders, so the decorating had to be minimal—something I could do without help.

The following Saturday morning, I dragged all the decorations to the front porch. When I looked up, I was surprised to see that everybody on the block was doing the same thing. Ladders leaned against just about every house, and lights were strewn across front lawns being untangled by family members. The heavy coats, scarves, and hats slowed the process, but at the same time, excitement and laughter permeated the street.

The men were calling out to one another about their work, and since there was no man in my house, I added my two cents to the mix. It was lighthearted banter, full of good cheer, and just what I needed.

It took me several hours to get my decorations up, but I still wasn't ready to go inside and miss getting to know my neighbors. Instead, I picked a house being decorated and introduced myself, adding a hand where needed. Soon, everyone had gathered at this house to help finish the decorating. We couldn't wait for evening, so we could view our creative designs.

That night, we met out front once again, enjoying the different decorations at each address. There was only one house on the block that wasn't decorated. The family who owned it was still in the process of moving in. I couldn't help noticing how lonesome the house looked.

Apparently, we all were noticing the same thing because the conversation soon switched to how we could help. In our excitement, everyone began talking at once. "I have leftover lights that go on bushes," said one neighbor. "I have a string of lights that might work on the porch," someone else added. "I have a yard scene that I can't use this year," said yet a different neighbor, "and I have a spotlight!"

It didn't take much persuading. We all agreed. We would surprise the new owners by turning their home into a Christmas card of welcome.

The next afternoon, we again met at one house and sorted through the leftover decorations. Together, we picked a theme and enough lights to cover the porch and garage. Even a timer was donated. Because they were in the process of moving in, the electricity had been turned on already, so we took the liberty of using the plug on the front porch and the donated timer. Within a short time, the home was decorated.

That night, as the lights came on at each of our homes, we again met in the middle of the street. This time the block was complete. The most beautifully decorated house was the one we had all worked on together. We couldn't wait for the new owners to bring their next load and see the surprise we'd created for them.

During the following week, I think everyone in the neighborhood kept one eye on the vacant house as we waited—rather impatiently—for the new neighbors to arrive. Then it happened. Toward the end of the week, a rental truck and two cars pulled into the driveway. The family and a couple of their friends got out of the vehicles and stood in the street. Their young children stared at their new home, now completely decorated, with awestruck eyes. They were speechless! Then they started jumping for joy.

One by one each neighbor came out and introduced themselves. Instant friendships were formed. We all helped unload the new family's belongings, and in a couple of hours they had all of their furniture in place and boxes in the correct rooms. As the new owners worked on the kitchen, several of us set up the beds. When all was said and done, the whole group went over to another neighbor's for hot drinks and cookies. Everyone agreed that we had the best decorations in the subdivision, bar none.

As we got to know the new neighbors better that evening, they shared their holiday wishes. Unbeknownst to us, their children had voiced only one holiday wish for Christmas that year: they wanted holiday lights on the outside of their house that would include *at least* one reindeer and a sleigh. It was a good feeling to know we had been instrumental in making that wish come true.

Ever since, we have continued to decorate our block for the holiday season. If by chance a new neighbor isn't prepared, we don't mind sharing what we have. We call it our Christmas Tradition for the Son. After all, he *is* the reason for the season!

*"Place your Christmas wishes inside
a treasured bottle for safekeeping."*

BY J. TROY SEATE

Messages in a Bottle

At one point in my father's life, he was a milkman. The significance of that career, and how it related to my family's most revered Christmas tradition, was explained to me as soon as I was old enough to understand.

The story begins in 1940, not long before the war that changed our nation in so many ways. Back then, when someone new worked in your part of Cleburne, Texas, everyone eventually spotted him or her. The current new man—spotted in the neighborhood my future mother lived in—was the milkman. She spotted him as he hauled his delivery out of the milk truck at the house across the street and got a good look at him when he returned with the empties. When she told me the story, she explained that the milk bottles rattling in their metal cages sounded like music when he carried them, causing her heart to pound like that of a schoolgirl.

Things were simpler then, clearer somehow, and she just knew this young man in the shiny, crisp, white uniform was the man for her. There was but one thing to do, and that was to have *her* milk delivered. Not caring what the neighbors might say, she waved the sturdy young man to her porch, introduced herself, and made the proper arrangements.

On the occasion of his first delivery, Dad left an empty bottle along with Mom's two-quart order, a piece of paper curled out of its opening. Mother recalls how her heart beat wildly as she read that first note, so many years ago. It read: *Would you consider going out with your milkman?*

Would she!

Exactly six months from the day my father delivered the empty milk bottle with its bold message, it was my mother who was dressed in white. The man of her dreams waited at the altar, as she made her grand entrance into the town's oldest Christian church to marry him.

As a result of my father's first request, my parents had gotten their wish—each other. The tradition of writing down what you wanted for Christmas and dropping it into that same empty milk bottle began during their first year of marriage. My mother decorated the bottle with a small wreath and hand-painted sprigs of holly and mistletoe on its outer surface. The bottle was then displayed at the Thanksgiving table, allowing both of them a full month to ponder their gifts.

During my parent's second year of marriage, Mom's note held an unusual Christmas request. She asked my father for a child. She asked him the same thing for three years running. The result was the birth of one daughter, one son, and, on the fourth year, me.

My siblings and I looked forward to Thanksgiving almost as much as Christmas, for that's when the sugarplums could begin to dance in our heads. We were encouraged to ask for something that would be useful to all of us. That didn't seem like much fun to us kids, but we knew our Christmas goodies weren't restricted to our milk jar requests.

Our house was the center of activity at Thanksgiving. A wave of hungry relatives always materialized to appease their appetites and to place their Christmas desires on a small note and drop it into the bottle's glass tummy.

As I grew older, I realized that the reason our relatives loved to come to our house for Thanksgiving was as much about putting their note in the milk jar as it was about the food and giving thanks. One aunt told me that my parents' unusual custom represented the milk of human kindness rather than the actual giving of gifts. Judging by the family closeness that has continued all these years, and how my own children took to the custom, I guess my aunt was right.

Some of my older relatives had suffered greatly during the Depression and the war that followed. My mom and dad became a kind of rallying cry for family unity. Mom's tradition seemed to represent the idea that hopes and dreams were still possible and goodwill and the spirit of giving were never out of style.

After Dad passed away, my elderly mother seemed to treasure the oft-repeated ceremony all the more. It bridged any generation gap we might have experienced over the years and the tradition has now entered into its fourth generation.

Mother chose me to be the guardian of the Christmas bottle and its messages. "Our tradition has brought all of us many wonderful gifts," she reminded me. "The best of them has been those from the heart. The ones in which people ask for no more than love and goodwill." I assured her I would not let the custom die, no matter how silly it might seem to some and so far I haven't.

Much of the original enamel green and red paint my mother applied to the milk jar that first Christmas has now peeled away, but every Thanksgiving through Christmas it still occupies a place of honor in my house. The simple quart jar, representative of my parents' love for family and each other, now sits on a bright Christmas doily with a small wreath adorning its stubby neck.

The little hands of my grandchildren still drop their thoughtful notes into its mouth, hoping this magical container will make their Christmas dreams come true. And, on behalf of my parents, I see to it that they do.

"Welcome the Holy Family to your home on Christmas Eve by lining your driveway or walk with luminary lights."

BY JEAN HAYNIE STEWART

Christmas Eve Luminaria

"Look, honey, the city gave us paper bags and candles," I said to my husband, as I held out the items and note that accompanied them. "All we have to do is add sand, and line our walk and driveway with them on Christmas Eve."

He looked interested. "Why?"

"Well, it says here that it's for a traditional Mexican custom of lighting the way for the Holy Family. Everyone lights the candles at 7 P.M. and turns off their porch lights for an hour."

He nodded. "Sounds nice. Let's do it."

So, in the midst of preparing for Christmas in our new Mission Viejo home, with our four-month-old twin girls, we added Christmas Eve luminaries to our list.

Christmas Eve arrived and so did high winds. As fast as we set the bags down, the wind blew them over. Our newly landscaped yard had bushes that were barely as tall as the lunch-size bags. As 7 P.M. approached, we worried that the winds would cause the lit bags to catch on fire, perhaps scorching or even burning our new plants.

"We'll just have to stand out here with them," Bill said.

I could see he was right. So we bundled up the babies, put them in their strollers, and went outside to light the luminaria. We discovered that our neighbors, up and down the street, had made the same decision.

"I'm going to bring out some coffee and cookies," I said. "Will you keep an eye on the girls?"

"Sure. And bring some of that cider, too."

I piled Christmas cookies on a paper plate, poured coffee into a Thermos and cider into a pitcher, grabbed some festive napkins, and put it all on a large tray. We stood by our mailbox and offered the goodies to our neighbors, who gradually congregated in our driveway to talk, between running to rescue flaming paper bags.

The following year, we set a card table in our driveway and neighbors, now friends, brought goodies to add to our treats.

We tried not to laugh out loud as one of the children cried, "We have to go home, now! I hear Santa coming! Now, Mommy! Daddy, hurry!" What she'd heard were the bells we had tied to our cocker spaniel's collar, to help him sound festive, and also to keep track of him in the yard. No amount of coaxing could convince her that she was not going to miss Santa's visit if they stayed, so they went home, and we removed the bells.

The next year, we set up a long table with a red paper cloth and an urn of Farmer's Bishop—hot cider steeped with cinnamon and clove-studded oranges. It was a hit, along with my mother's famous sausage balls.

Through the years, our evening festivities grew. Our neighbors placed large red candles in an elaborate candelabra and then ceremoniously marched down the middle of the street, carrying it to our table. We set up outside speakers and played Christmas carols, and another neighbor won the home decorating contest. Those who drove by to see the lights often stopped for a cup of cider and a cookie, as if it were part of the tour.

As our children grew and our community friendships broadened, so did our invitations. Folks from school and church stopped by on their way to or from services, or dinner, bringing out-of-town guests with them and always a plate of something for the table.

"It's the perfect way to have a party," I commented. "Because we're outside, the house stays neat and ready for Christmas Day!"

That statement was true, until the girls became teenagers and their friends made our luminaria part of their Christmas Eve celebration, too.

As my mother went through the house one year, on her way to refill a tray, she returned to the chilly night and pulled her coat around her, murmuring, "Why do the kids have enough sense to go inside, while we stand out here in the cold?"

I looked at her querulously, before going inside to check. Sure enough, there they were, sprawled on the floor in front of the blazing fireplace, laughing and enjoying the time, free from adults and younger children. "Smart," I thought, and quietly returned outside.

It had to happen—one year it rained. The luminary bags were soggy messes along the driveways. Everyone piled into our not-too-large house, bringing their Christmas cheer with them.

Twenty-five years passed and our daughters graduated from college and married. When we flew to be with one of them at Christmas, we canceled luminaria for the first time. On our return, a friend told us, "It was awful. We had to bring our own coffee and stand in your driveway and just stare at each other." He was kidding, of course—I think.

With time, children grew; families began to travel to be with their grown children and grandchildren and our guest list dwindled. We now attend our granddaughter's church Nativity pageant instead of serving cider in the driveway. Life is full of changes. But the memories remain and we still receive Christmas cards that mention the happy memories of our driveway luminaria. And today, before we leave the house on Christmas Eve, we turn on our new electric luminaries. We don't want the Holy Family to lose their way.

> *"Nothing makes the holiday more special than spending time with grandparents."*

BY PAM GIORDANO

Nona, Nuts, and Nostalgia

I feel exceedingly privileged to have lived among ethnic neighborhoods. There was always an excuse for a party—a celebration of this new country, perhaps, or of some saint from a village in the old country who deserved recognition. There were banners and flags and music, and plenty of the best of each country's favorite dishes. I looked forward to each celebration, but none could compete with my Italian grandmother's Christmas.

My family lived in a town several miles away from my grandparents' home. Each year, from the time I was ten, my father drove me to Grammy's a few days before the holiday, so I could help her prepare for the upcoming event. I understood that Christmas would not focus on gift giving. Our grandparents believed only in the gifts of family and food. They did, however, prepare a shoebox full of treats for each of their grandchildren. Inside was everything we could imagine: fruit, nuts, chewing gum, and—if my grandfather was in a benevolent mood from too much wine—a quarter wrapped in a piece of waxed paper!

The first time I joined in on the preparation, I felt tentative and slightly threatened by the large assortment of fruits, vegetables, and nuts that Grandpop had collected on his trip to Philadelphia.

"You wash your hands; then we start the nuts," Grammy ordered, as she tied one of her large white aprons around my waist. Then she put a large amount of almonds on a long cookie sheet and led me to the coal stove. "Watch, no burn. If you make too dark, nuts get bitter—no good," she announced, as she showed me how to carefully shove the nuts around with my fingers. I didn't leave the stove for a second. It was an important job, and I didn't want my mother to hear that I was the one responsible for burning the nuts.

By the time I was finished at the stove, Grammy had the grinder clamped to the side of the table. "Now," she said, "you grind. Put some nuts, some figs, a little bit orange skin and do again."

I did as I was instructed, but the result was a sorry-looking mess. I couldn't believe that we were actually going to eat the stuff.

"What's this for, Grammy?" I asked, suspiciously.

"For the cookies!" Grammy answered, as if she thought I should know. "You see! I gonna make pretty soon. Now, you go downstairs and bring me prosciutto."

I loved going down into the cellar. It was smelly, dark, and damp, filled with Grandpop's wine barrels and all manner of mysterious things. I found Grandpop's bench and reached up to where the prosciutto was hanging from a hook on a beam. I learned that it was from a pig that Grandpop had chosen himself. Grammy took the ham from me and, with a brush, scrubbed the outside, removing the white stuff that clung to it. It would be my lunch for tomorrow.

When Grammy was finished, she mixed my sorry-looking mess into a pot on the stove, adding jam and chocolate and other spices. Soon, a wonderful aroma was wafting through the house.

"You taste," Grammy said, as she shoved a spoonful of filling into my mouth. *It was wonderful!* "Tomorrow," she continued, "I finish the cookie and you go to market and chicken store."

I made a face, showing my utter displeasure at having to go into the disgusting chicken store. "But Grammy . . ."

She held up her hand to stop me. "You go to market and to chicken store. I give you money for movie after," she said with a smile. The offer made things a bit more palatable, but I still swallowed hard when I thought about entering that dreadfully smelly place. Thinking I'd be off the hook, I prayed for snow. After all, what grandmother would send her special child out in horrible weather? I underestimated her resolve. The next morning, despite a new layer of snow, Grammy would hear no protests.

"You put boots," she said calmly. "Watch, no fall. Go to market and tell Mr. Messina you want five big artichoke. Tell him no take from bottom. He always put best ones on top. You tell him you want from top! Then, you go to chicken store. Tell lady you want two big hen. Tell her no take out eggs from inside. I need for soup." And then, as if all of that was not enough, she added, "You stop at church. Father Perlo hear your confession."

I smiled broadly. *I was safe.* I had just been to confession. "Grammy, I went to confession three days ago," I announced. "I don't need to go again."

My grandmother raised her voice and her rolling pin. "No need?" she asked, in disbelief. "No need blessing? You stop at church. Tell Father Perlo, you Nona say you need!" Then as if her displeasure wasn't enough, she threatened me. "No blessing, no movie!"

That afternoon, I, the dutiful child, exhausted and free of all sin, sat through the news, three previews, one serial, one cartoon, and a double-feature—my reward for going to the chicken store, which turned out to be okay, once I learned to hold my breath. I leaned back in my seat and opened the little bag Grammy had given me. Inside, I found a delicious prosciutto sandwich, fresh cookies, and a blood orange—my reward for a job well done.

Each year, I returned to Grammy's. Each year, I was the one who toasted the nuts and ground the ingredients for the cookies. And each year, Grammy let me assume more and more of the cooking responsibility, until I was good enough to make the cookies on my own. I continued to go into the basement for the prosciutto and, when I didn't need the bench any longer and Grandpop was gone, I used it anyway. It was my way of keeping him with us for the holiday. Each year, I dutifully returned to the chicken store. The smell never got any better, but I eventually became an expert on deep breaths.

The chicken store is now a Laundromat, and I no longer go to matinees with prosciutto sandwiches or confess to Father Perlo. Grammy is gone and, with her, many of the traditions of the old country. But each Christmas, as I toast the almonds, I raise a glass in honor of the one who helped me make Christmas the best celebration of them all.

"Buon Natale, Nona!"

"Put a smile on the faces of your loved ones. Pack them into the family car and take a spin. There is much magic to be seen in the festival of lights dripping from trees and porch eaves all around town."

BY CONNIE VIGIL PLATT

Happy Memories and Bright Futures

When my children were little, money was practically nonexistent.

My husband was attending college on the GI Bill, and we were willing to sacrifice a little now for a better life later. Although we were broke, we didn't consider ourselves poor. Everyone we knew was broke. Along with all our friends, we had learned to make do with simple pleasures. We went to each other's houses for card games and coffee, the kids all played together, and everybody got along.

Because we wanted to give our children happy memories along with a brighter future, we all became quite creative during the holidays.

In the college town we lived in, work was hard to find, so I was a stay-at-home mom. I was pretty handy with a needle though and made as many Christmas presents as possible, including doll clothes, pajamas, and shirts. I always made enough to give to children in our circle of friends as well. I was recycling hand-me-downs long before it was popular. I remember fondly how I used to stay up alone and work late into the night, so I could hide my efforts until the big day. My husband, too, offered his best, making wooden toys for the boys in his spare time. By cutting corners and working long hours in secret, we always had some money set aside and tried to purchase at least one special toy that our children had asked for.

I baked cookies and made candy and popcorn balls. The kids helped with the decorating, putting on sprinkles and nuts or whatever we found in the cupboard. During the holidays, the entire house smelled like cinnamon and molasses, and we always had a tree festooned with tinsel and lights. A girlfriend even showed me how to make ornaments out of old cans, which were kind of cute. With children in the house, Christmas Eve is always special, even when there isn't any money.

After the newscaster announced that Santa's sleigh had been spotted over Iceland, or some other distant place, he'd add that Santa and his reindeer were being escorted by fighter planes, just to be sure they made it through the night safely. We all watched the newscast anxiously—our children's eyes wide—as the radar showed little blips indicating Santa and eight tiny reindeer sailing across the television screen. By that time, the children were so excited they wouldn't be able to sleep! To make the magic last longer, we bundled them up and drove around the neighborhood, enjoying the lights and decorated houses of the people who *weren't* worried about their electricity bill, at least for this month. By the time we got back home, the children were always relaxed enough to sleep.

This evening as my husband, Claude, and I reminisced about past Christmases, we smiled, remembering the good times. As a family, we had made that yearly pilgrimage even in bad weather. One year, the snow plow didn't come through until late in the afternoon. Thankfully it came in time for us to take the children on their yearly trip around town to see the lights.

Of course, it was late when we got back home that Christmas Eve. My husband and I were up much later than the children that evening. We had to track down all the places we had hidden the gifts our children would find under the tree in the morning. But that, too, was part of the fun.

We continued this effortless tradition until the children grew up and were on their own. Even after we could afford more luxuries, we still enjoyed driving around town and viewing the bright porches and front lawns.

My husband and I still go out for a drive on Christmas Eve. It seems the decorations get more elaborate every year. And every year we say that next year we'll put up our own decorations, but we never do. That might change our need to drive through town leisurely on Christmas Eve to enjoy the efforts of others, and we'd rather leave our tradition intact.

This year, as we prepared for our annual drive on Christmas Eve, I was pleasantly surprised when the phone rang. It was our daughter calling from across the continent to wish us Merry Christmas.

"I can't talk long," she said, "we're getting ready to take the kids to go see the Christmas lights."

I smiled, thinking we were about to do the same.

I heard the excitement in her voice as she continued. "Do you remember how much fun we used to have doing that, driving around town even if the weather was bad?"

I do remember, and I told her so.

"Was the snow really deeper when we were little?" she asks. Without waiting for an answer, she rushes into the next sentence, and I can tell she is reliving her childhood this evening through the excitement of her own children, much as my husband and I used to do. "I get the kids all bundled up like you used to do with us, and by the time we get home they're ready for bed." She laughed lightheartedly, and I felt the warmth of her smile through the phone lines. "Like we used to be."

I smiled and pondered her questions. *It had always been that much fun back then.* I shifted, so that my gaze took in my husband as he bundled up in his coat and gloves. His big happy smile as he pulled on his hat said it all. *It had always been that much fun and it would continue to be that much fun—even if it was just the two of us.*

"Yes, the snow really was deeper when you were little," I said into the receiver, as I reached for my husband's hand. "Your father and I were just now getting ready to go see the lights ourselves."

"Everybody loves a parade—

especially a Christmas parade!"

BY DIXON HEARNE

The Rudolph Sweater

Though the sun ducked behind a bank of gray clouds, where it remained the rest of the week, I didn't complain. The chilly air and cozy comforts brought an early dose of Christmas Spirit to our town. Before my very eyes, bedazzled trees sprang up in picture windows, and festive streamers and garlands appeared on busy streets and storefronts. Thanksgiving herbs had not faded and dispersed but rather blended into the lively smells of Christmas—cinnamon, clove, peppermint, lemon zest, and evergreen resins.

It was that wonderful time of year again.

As everyone knew, the annual Christmas Parade ushered in the official start of holiday shopping. We could hardly wait. Right down the center of town came the marching bands and majorettes tossing batons like propellers into the air, interspersed with some thirty colorful floats headed up by the mayor and city council. Old Mr. and Mrs. Stackhouse, always dressed up in western attire, waved "Howdy" from their very own authentic stagecoach festooned with loops of garland tied with silver bows. Young cowboys in red and green Stetson hats trailed along behind them, twirling their lassos into the hearts and imaginations of onlookers. And the sounds of the season—from Bing Crosby to sing-along carols and kiddy tunes—resonated through the streets. The air was magic with hope and longing. We felt special just to be there, to witness the celebration, and to become part of it.

My best friend, Scotty, and I pushed and tugged and stood our own ground at the front of the crowd for a long while—till a rowdy high school boy decided to shove me headlong into the middle of a marching band. I was petrified!

"Stop still!" a burly band member yelled at me. "Stop and wait till we pass!"

Spectators gawked and pointed, and I froze in place, until the drum row finally passed. But quick on their heels was the next float, flanked on both sides by uniformed police cadets, marching lock-step and heavy.

"Up here!" A loud voice called from the enormous float designed like a train engine, with the words *Christmas Special* emblazoned along its sides. "Give me your hand, boy! Jump!"

There was no time to think better of it. I leapt with all my strength and grasped two reaching arms that jerked me onboard as effortlessly as if it had been rehearsed. The crowd began to cheer, flashing smiles in my direction. Even the hateful bully, who had shoved me, gave me two thumbs up—and instantaneously, I became a sort of parade mascot for the remainder of the long trip down DeSiard Street. Indeed, it would take more than a prank to spoil the parade.

With the passing smiles and hand-waving and voices calling out my name, I felt special for the first time in my life, even famous for a brief moment. I waved back, nervous and awkward, but I knew instinctively it was my moment, a time that would be forever etched in my heart and mind.

As always, the parade would eventually disperse in each direction at Five Points, driven ever forward by the brassy sounds of "Here Comes Santa Claus" from the rear, while Santa and his helpers tossed lollipops to the reaching crowd. Some folks took to the street behind his sleigh and followed along to where Santa was quickly spirited away before suspecting children could investigate.

My mother and aunt had waited patiently at Five Points for the parade's end, at which time we were to meet up again. The look of surprise that registered on their faces when they saw me waving from the Rotary float was a bona fide Kodak moment if ever there was one. I got to see the celebration from both sides now—spectator and participant. I would later conclude that I really liked each equally well. It was also the first time I can actually recall being thankful for my mother's insistence on holiday dress. Today, that Rudolph sweater she'd made me wear seemed somehow quite appropriate!

"Choose a special set of silverware to use for Christmas dinner and pass it on in the family as you would a precious heirloom."

BY TERRI TIFFANY

Silver Linings

When I grew up in the sixties, my mother worked full-time. She wasn't often around to help our family create traditions—except at Christmastime. On that holiday, she turned into June Cleaver and, as one of three daughters, I was kept busy with duties throughout the day.

"Terri, it's time to set the table," Mother announced, as she wiped her hands on the dishtowel tucked into her waistband. The scent of roast turkey filled our tiny kitchen. She reached for a fork to stir the gravy boiling on top of the stove, while I hurried into the dining room to open the buffet drawer.

Before she married, my mother saved money, earned from her job as a secretary at a feed mill, to purchase her first set of silverware. Wrapped in rich velvet, a complete set of utensils became her dowry, when she married my father a year later. The faded receipt still lay folded in the back pouch of the lid, attesting to the magnitude of my mother's hopes. On Christmas Day, I enjoyed the privilege of removing each piece from its lined bed to set around the holiday table like jewels on a queen.

I loved to caress the fine workmanship, as I placed the pieces beside my mother's good china. I dreamed of the day I would be a bride, planning for my future, like my mother before me. Year after year, I pulled the forks and knifes from hibernation to make our Christmas table sparkle with magic and memories.

After I married and returned home for Christmas, I always hurried to the same drawer. "I'll set the table, Mom. Can we use the good silver?" Of course, she nodded. It wasn't Christmas, until the gravy ladle and carving knife rested in their places and the weighted metal molded to our hands.

When I became a mother, and Christmas meant remaining closer to home, the trips to my parents' house dwindled. But every time I visited, I reminded my mother about the silverware.

Last year, we returned home to visit my father, who was now confined to a nursing home. After we said our goodbyes to him, my husband and I drove Mother back to my childhood home, which now echoed with emptiness. I couldn't even remember the last Christmas I'd spent at home with my parents. As I gazed at the familiar kitchen, I wished for one more morning with my father turning on the Christmas lights and my mother shoving the stuffed turkey into the oven.

"We'll try to come home this year for Christmas, if we can, Mom," I said.

"I want you to have something now, in case you don't," she replied. Silently, she rose from the chair. I watched as she opened the buffet drawer and withdrew the chest I loved so much. "Can you take this home with you now?"

I knew what she was asking. Despite my desire for the object that defined my Christmas, I understood the significance of the moment.

When she passed the silver to me, many of my mother's own Christmas traditions would end.

She smiled gently. "You always were the one to remember to use them. The other girls never cared, but I know you did."

One last time, she unfolded the faded receipt and stroked each piece of silverware.

"We never did figure out what this piece was for, did we?" she laughed, as she turned over a slotted implement, while I scanned the manufacturer's booklet.

"A pastry turner," I said at last, and smiled at the thought. "I doubt the pumpkin pies missed it."

Mom grinned. Then she closed the lid with a soft click and placed the treasure in my arms.

Every now and then, I pull a piece of my mother's silver from its new home in my buffet drawer and gaze at it reverently. The tinkling of forks, as my sisters and I shared our Christmas dinner with my parents fills my memories. Then I tuck the fabric back around the silverware set, eager for the holiday when I begin making new memories with my own growing family.

"Create your own Christmas Village.
Start with one house and add a new
item to the village each year."

BY JUNETTE KIRKHAM WOLLER

The Mirror Pond

"Come on, Judy, this is where we get off."

As we stepped off the bus, Mother held tightly to my hand. As the Gulf winter wind swirled around the downtown Galveston buildings, it stung my eyes and cheeks. Christmas street decorations did a windy dance to the Salvation Army Santa's bell, as store window lights blinked off and on.

We headed for McCrory's Five- and Ten-Cent Store. Sailors with their collars turned up and their hands shoved into the pockets of their pea coats hurried past us. I felt sad, knowing they probably wouldn't be home for Christmas.

We stopped for a few moments in front of a store window that displayed mechanical moving scenes. Elves painted toys, and Santas laughed holding their bellies. The more elaborate windows depicted scenes from *The Nutcracker*. Even with the cold, magic filled the air.

Warmth enveloped us as we entered the store. I felt in the pocket of my red wool coat to make certain the dollar I had saved was still there. There were several presents I wanted to buy. The one special thing I wanted to look for, though, was another figure to add to my mirror pond. Every year, Mother let me take a small mirror, put it on the floor beneath the Christmas tree, and make a winter scene. I would take my time, arranging and rearranging, until everything looked just right.

"Let's go to the linen department to look for a tablecloth," said Mother. "Then we'll do your shopping."

We wove our way through the crowd, our footsteps making hollow sounds on the wooden floor. Mother sorted through the tablecloths but wasn't satisfied with any of them.

She sighed. "I suppose we'll have to go to Eiband's." Eiband's Department Store was more expensive, and I knew we didn't have a lot of money. Even so, I liked walking through that store and looking at all the pretty things.

"We'll do your shopping first," Mother said, grabbing my hand as we shouldered our way back through the crowd to the variety counters. When we got there, Mother browsed nearby, letting me shop by myself. I decided to look at the handkerchiefs first. They always made nice gifts. I kept my milk money for school tied in a corner of my handkerchief.

This year, I was finally tall enough to see over the wooden display counter. Pieces of glass separated the handkerchiefs into sections for men, women, and children. I selected a plain white one for my father for ten cents. A pink one with an embroidered rose in one corner would be perfect for the pocket of Mother's nurse uniform. I gave the lady behind the counter my dollar. She put each handkerchief in its own box with tissue paper, put the boxes in a paper bag, and then handed me the bag and seventy cents.

I had two things left to purchase, a present for my little brother and my mirror-pond figure. I walked along the wooden counters until

I came to the toys. Everything I thought my brother would like cost more than the dollar I used to have. Cars, trucks, and cap pistols with holsters were all too expensive. I sighed and took one more look. Way at the back of the counter, I spied a small red fire engine. As I stood on tiptoe, trying to reach it, the saleswoman picked it up and placed it in my hand.

"Thank you," I said remembering my manners, "I would like to buy this for my little brother for Christmas. Would you please tell me how much it costs?"

The lady smiled. "That particular fire engine costs fifty cents."

I quickly did the math in my head. Fifty cents from seventy cents would leave me with twenty cents. Maybe that would be enough for a small figure of some sort.

"I'll take it, please." I handed her fifty cents. She wrapped the fire engine in tissue paper, put it into a paper bag, and handed it to me.

"Are you finished shopping now?" Mother asked, as she stepped up to the counter.

I shook my head. "I have one more thing to get," I said, as I looked around at the other counters. Finally, I saw the one with all kinds of figurines and began searching for something I could afford. Ceramic flowers, birds, and butterflies filled most of the counter. None of them looked suitable for my winter scene. I sighed and started to turn away, when a saleswoman asked if I was looking for something special.

"Yes, ma'am, I'm trying to find a small figure for my Christmas winter scene. I only have twenty cents left."

She smiled. "I think I have just the thing for you," she said, as she reached down among the birds. Carefully, she pulled out a tiny delicate swan. "Would this do?"

"Oh, yes," I sighed, as I gazed at the delicate bird. "But how much is it?"

"Let me see," she said. Tipping the bird upside down, she read the sticker price on the bottom. "It's exactly fifteen cents. May I wrap it up for you?"

"Yes, please," I said, handing her a dime and a nickel.

With packages in hand, and a nickel in my pocket, we went to Eiband's for the tablecloth. Mother quickly found what she wanted, and we headed back out into the cold just in time to catch our bus.

Daddy had set up our Christmas tree in the living room. All we had to do was get the decorations out of the closet.

"When can we decorate the tree?" I asked, anxious to get started on my pond scene.

"Go next door and bring your brother home," Mother instructed. "Daddy should be home soon. He can get the boxes of decorations, while I fix dinner. After we eat, we can all decorate the tree."

Throughout the meal, my little brother chattered about Christmas and what he wanted from Santa. All I could think about was my mirror pond. Later, when I helped Mother clear the table, Daddy brought out the boxes of decorations.

While the rest of the family decorated the tree, I sorted through my box of figurines. As soon as Mother finished putting the cotton around the tree base, I made a space in it for the mirror and carefully hid the edge. After I fluffed up the cotton to look like mounds of snow, I positioned three tiny artificial evergreens around it to create a small forest. The tiny house would go next to one of the trees, and then it would be time to scatter the little glass animals; a squirrel, a rabbit, a red bird, a doe, and a fawn. Last of all, I placed the swan on the pond.

"Time to light the tree," said Mother, from across the room.

I quickly joined my family and waited for the thrill of seeing our tree light up. Standing back to get a good view, we watched Daddy plug in the cord. Everything looked so beautiful! The glass ornaments reflected different colors and the tinsel sparkled magnificently! Even our handmade ornaments looked special.

Just over my mirror pond was a blue light. It made the whole scene look cold and wintery. It was perfect! I glanced at my little brother whose eyes were bright. The smile on his face filled the room with joy and excitement. This would be another wonderful Christmas for all of us.

"Let no distance separate you and the ones you love during the holidays."

BY CHARLIE HUDSON

An Ocean Apart

In 1991, a few weeks after my son Dustin's tenth birthday, his stepfather and I both received alert orders for deployment from Germany to Desert Shield / Desert Storm. The orders were simple: Go to Saudi Arabia and you'll come home when the war is over.

Due to a previous army assignment, we had only been reunited as a family for a few months. Unfortunately, we had no means of keeping Dustin and our longtime live-in sitter in Germany. After some discussion, we decided that Dustin would go to Maine for the month of December to be with his paternal grandparents and then to Houston in January to stay with my sister. Her son was a few years older than Dustin and the cousins were close. Dustin's father had been killed in an accident when he was four months old, and even though he loved his grandparents, we felt it would be better for him to be with his male cousin.

The sitter would accompany him to Maine, where Dustin would bid farewell to a woman who had been like a second mother to him for more than three years. When I said goodbye to them at the Frankfurt airport, none of us knew if we would see each other again.

Unlike today, communication from the Persian Gulf was extremely difficult. I received a few letters and wrote many more, yet it was not until later that I learned Dustin's grandfather had suffered an unexpected heart attack at home in February and died without regaining consciousness. Although my parents traveled from Louisiana to Texas to break the news to him, it was a tragic blow to a child already coping with having both parents in a war zone.

Happily, Desert Storm ended quickly and we were a family again by June 1991. Due to the postwar reduction in the Armed Forces, we were to be reassigned from Germany to Italy. As luck would have it, I was required to go to Italy ahead of my husband and Dustin. At least this time it was only a month-long separation. Less than two weeks after my departure, Dustin awakened my husband, complaining of stomach pains, which turned out to be acute appendicitis. Though there were no complications from the surgery, it was not an ideal way to spend Thanksgiving.

Thankfully, I was allowed to rush back to apply some mothering. During one bedtime conversation, Dustin asked about Christmas. From the time he had been a baby, we'd either spent Christmas with his grandparents in Maine or they delayed Christmas until his arrival a few days after the holiday.

"Gram shouldn't have to spend this Christmas alone, not without Grandpa," he said softly. I agreed and quickly explained that I already asked Gram to visit us for the holidays.

Although I had been certain I could persuade her to come, Gram was reluctant to leave her home and her pets in the middle of winter or to make a transatlantic journey alone. I understood her reasoning but also understood what a difficult Christmas it would be without her husband or any other family. Dustin's father had been their only child,

Grandpa had no brothers or sisters, and Gram's only brother had died in his youth.

"Well," Dustin suggested tentatively, "maybe we could all go there."

As much as my heart went out to the idea of Gram alone in a Maine winter, it was simply not possible for us to break away for a week. As gently as I could, I explained that to my young son.

Hardly a minute passed before Dustin looked at me with serious eyes. "Then can I go be with her?"

I shook my head sadly. "Sweetheart, that means you would have to fly by yourself and it would be just a week before you'd have to come back to school."

"That's okay," he said earnestly. "I don't mind, really. I don't want Gram to be by herself."

I leaned forward and kissed him good night. "Get some sleep and let me think about it," I whispered, too astounded to know what else to say.

That night my husband and I discussed it. Dustin was a remarkably experienced traveler, having flown from age one and also having flown unaccompanied since the age of five. In fact, he'd flown unaccompanied from Atlanta to London, when he rejoined us after Desert Storm, a mere six months before. Granted, we were in the process of moving to Italy, but they had direct flights, didn't they?

In the end, we drove to Switzerland and flew Dustin direct from Zurich to Portland, Maine, where he arrived December 27th for a late Christmas with his beloved grandmother. When I called to tell her of the plan, she protested: Dustin was barely eleven, it was winter, and she would be fine. At that point, I turned the telephone over to Dustin. He insisted it was his idea and that he would be very unhappy if she didn't want him to come.

Not want him to? How could she say no?

And so it was that Dustin kept a tradition that he has continued no matter where we were assigned. He traveled alone from Italy once again a year or so later, and then twice from Hawaii, before we finally returned to the East Coast.

Dustin is no longer a child. These days he juggles his own hectic schedule. But come Christmas Eve, or within a day or two of that most special holiday, you can be sure Dustin will be unwrapping presents at Gram's house.

BY LISA FINCH

A New Tradition

Outside, the gray sky mirrored my mood. January 6th, the day of the Epiphany or Little Christmas, meant time to take down the Christmas tree. With a heavy heart, I lugged the boxes from the furnace room and prepared to remove the decorations. My husband, Chris, stood on a stool and began taking the strands of lights from the tree. As I reached for one of the shiny baubles, I thought of Nana and how blue she used to be when it was time to say goodbye to the tree for another year.

One ornament, hanging near the top of the tree, glistened beyond my reach. I asked Chris to get it down for me, as I knelt at the foot of the tree, retrieving the bulbs off the lower branches. Glancing up, I looked at the silver and blue ornament in his hand. It was one of a kind, given to me by Nana.

"Catch," Chris said, pretending to toss it to me.

"Don't you dare!" I snapped.

"Got it?" Chris asked, as he dropped it into my hand. But I didn't have it. We both watched helplessly, as it bounced off my palm and smashed into a million pieces. I gasped at the little shards of silver glinting among the Berber carpet. In despair, I looked up at Chris, his face stricken. Our seven-year-old son, Ben, ran to us, his eyes huge.

My vision blurred with tears as I looked at what was left of my precious gift.

"Mom, what is it?" Ben asked.

"Mom's ornament—that she had since she was five," Chris said as he climbed down from the step-stool, his arms hanging at his sides. "I broke it."

Childhood memories of helping Nana set up her ancient artificial tree loomed before me. Each year, right after Halloween, Uncle Drew and I started pestering Nana about Christmas decorating. She always put up a fight, saying it was too early. But we saw through her half-hearted protests, and she knew it. She wanted to start the festivities almost as early as we did. By mid-November, she'd had enough of our pleading and quietly relented.

Only twelve years my senior and more big brother than uncle, Drew delighted in Christmas. The earlier and the more Christmas the better, seemed to be his way when it came to his favorite season. I can still picture him coming in from hanging the exterior Christmas lights, face red from the cold, but still singing Christmas carols with gusto!

Then we'd cart all those musty cartons and boxes out of the attic crawlspace in his room. Each year a few more bulbs had shattered from the heat. Without air-conditioning, the summer wreaked havoc on Nana's delicate glass ornaments.

After decorating, the three of us sang Christmas carols by the softly colored lights on the tree, further illuminated by silver "snowflake" tinsel that adorned the branches. Every year, Nana said the same thing, as she gazed at our treasure, "This is the prettiest tree ever!"

Nana and Drew are both gone now, but Nana's happy words continue to ring in my head. The sad part was that the only thing I had left from Nana's house was that five-inch ornament with its stripes of blue, silver, and white. That one little Christmas ornament had held a lifetime of Christmas memories for me.

Each year, as we set up our tree, my family jokingly groaned as I explained the significance of that bulb for the umpteenth time. As Ben looked saw my tears, he cried with me. "Maybe we can get a new one," he said, taking my hand.

I shook my head. "We can't. It's the last one from Nana's tree. There aren't any more like it."

"I'm so sorry," Chris said, as the three of us hugged, trying to heal our hurt.

After a few minutes, I sent Ben back to his video game. In silence, Chris and I finished taking down the tree and putting away the remaining ornaments.

When we were finished, Chris looked at me. "Lisa, I really am sorry."

"I know," I replied. "It was an accident. It's just that . . . it's the only thing I had from Nana's house. Now I have nothing. Not even pictures."

Nana didn't have much, and what she did have mysteriously disappeared after she died. No one in the family seemed to know what happened to the boxes of cards, photos, and postcards my grandfather had sent her during World War II.

I picked up the shards in the carpet, and remembered the sad expression on Nana's face when we took the tree down. "All over for another year," she'd say sadly. *In this case, all over forever.* I pictured Nana carefully putting away all those ornaments, grateful for the ones that had made it through another season.

At his video game, Ben started to cry again.

"Ben, what is it?" I asked.

"I just can't stop thinking about how sad you are."

"Okay, I won't be sad anymore," I said, as I pulled him into my arms. "You're sweet to be so concerned about me."

"We could look for another one," he suggested again.

I stooped down and looked into his face. "Tell you what, Ben. We'll start a new tradition. We'll go shopping together, and we'll pick out a new ornament."

Ben's round face grew hopeful.

I shrugged. "It won't be exactly the same, but maybe it will be close."

"It might be the same," he said, his eyes shining.

Maybe. I smiled. After all, Christmas is a time for magic. And I knew for sure there were two people in heaven who would guide us to the right place and the perfect ornament to begin our new tradition.

"In order to believe in Santa Claus, every child needs a visit from him on Christmas Eve. Won't you be Santa this year?"

BY LINDA MEHUS-BARBER

No Wonder I Believe

Half a century is a long time, yet when I allow my mind to drift back to childhood it seems like an out-of-body experience, as vivid as if it had happened just yesterday.

I zoom in on Alberta, in western Canada. Didsbury. The west side of the tracks. And there it is: a simple, two-story, wood-sided house. I wander into the kitchen and am enveloped by the aroma of tomorrow's dinner. Mom bustles about, preparing a thirty-pound turkey, while cinnamon-spiced cranberries simmer on the back burner.

In the living room, Dad lies on the brown leather recliner, with the *Calgary Herald* open and spread over his chest—the hint of a snore suggests a slip into slumber. The needle on the record player scratches out the Big Band sounds of Tommy Dorsey, while a freshly cut spruce stands in a corner guarding brightly wrapped bundles, its twinkling lights reflected in the window.

There I am, at age seven, kneeling on the overstuffed Chesterfield, haunches on heels, chin cradled in cupped hands, staring out the window. I loved sitting on the couch like that; it was my favorite spot. I peer through the veranda, over the rail, toward the gnarled, but fruitful, mountain ash. A flock of cedar waxwings teeter on the leafless branches, feasting on the fermented scarlet berries the tree provides during harsh prairie winters. Snowflakes—those magical crystals sent down from heaven—glisten like diamonds in the soft light.

Back then, it always snowed on Christmas Eve. Mom said it was so Santa wouldn't have to worry about landing or taking off. And Santa was real—I knew he was because Mom said so.

As evening wore on, I waited anxiously for the knock on the door I knew would come. My heart leaped when the staccato rap I'd been waiting for finally sounded. Even though I diligently watched, I never saw Santa approach the house—he was that magical! Flanked by my three younger brothers and feeling like my insides were ready to burst, I sprang up and flew to the kitchen to peek around the corner as Dad went to answer the door.

When Dad flung the door wide, I knew who I would see. I was never disappointed. Sure enough! There was the man in the red suit! His snowy beard, ruddy cheeks, and twinkling blue eyes were right off the pages of my favorite Christmas picture book!

Every year, without fail, Santa visited our house to signal bedtime and to give us new pajamas for what seemed like the longest night of the year. He visited all the other houses on the street, too. I had no reason not to believe he visited every house in the world—Mom said he did.

Smoke from Dad's pipe curled above his head, as he motioned us toward Santa to receive our flannel bundles. I never once wondered why Mom wasn't there to partake of the big event. I was just so excited to see Santa, I couldn't think of anything else.

As the last "Ho, ho, ho!" faded into the night, my brothers and I scurried up the stairs, quickly changed into our new pajamas, and snuggled into bed. Santa had told us he'd be back once we were asleep—and *if* we were asleep when he returned, he said he'd bring more than PJs!

I fluffed my feather pillow and dropped my head into it, blonde curls tangled in a heap. Mom came up a little later to pray with me and to plant a gentle good-night kiss on my forehead. Thus, another typical Christmas Eve passed into memory.

Over the years, Mom and Dad grew grey. After a while the big city with all its hustle and bustle became our home, and my little brothers grew taller than me. One day, while looking for our family photo album, I lifted the lid of Mom's cedar chest and made a surprise discovery. There, on the top of her treasures was an old velvet Santa suit. A weathered harness of genuine sleigh bells tucked in beside it.

As my mouth dropped open, I sensed Mom slip into the room behind me. Turning toward her, I saw a radiant smile slowly spread across her face, erasing the years of wear. I choked back tears, as I finally understood why she had never been there when Santa came. For Mom, Christmas Eve meant running up and down the silent street making the spirit of St. Nick real for all the neighborhood children— not just her own.

No wonder I believe.

> *"Christmas memories linger long after special wrapping paper has been set aside and gifts put away. Those memories grow stronger when Grandma uses the same special box—year after year—to wrap gifts for her loved ones."*

BY LAURA S. WHITE

The Special Box

C hristmas has always been a time for making memories and for laughter and joy. Programs, concerts, and great get-togethers centering around the holiday are all ingrained to make the Christmas season the most cherished of the year. People hustle and bustle as they shop. Strangers call "Merry Christmas." Snow falls softly, creating a festive atmosphere. And as we age, memories of previous Christmases come to mind, holidays when those we loved—whose places at the table now remain empty—helped create our most lasting traditions.

We didn't know we were creating a tradition the Christmas a very special wrapping box was introduced to our family festivities. As we wrapped a gift for one of the grandkids, we had no idea it would etch a lasting picture in our minds. To complete the gift, holiday paper was wrapped around the pretty box, concealing the picture painted on it, and a bow was added.

Christmas morning came, and the family arrived at Grandma's house with all the noise and excitement that four children can bring. Between the kids and the dog that magical holiday morning, we adults had to work hard to salvage what little sanity we had left. Though Mom and I shared her home, it was always known as Grandma's House. It was a special place, where family bonding began and where it will continue from one generation to the next. I helped Mom as much as I could, so that she could be the grandma the kids would remember, and she made special efforts to create memories for them that would carry throughout their lifetimes.

As was her tradition, we ate the Christmas meal before any gifts were shared. The children were excited, of course, and if they were anything like I had been as a child, I'm sure there were many years when they weren't even aware of what was being served!

Dishes were washed quickly and leftovers put away, so the family could gather on the enclosed porch, around the Christmas tree. Everyone always sat in the same spot, with the kids claiming the floor. We took turns opening one gift at a time, going from youngest to oldest, so we could all see and share in the excitement and joy.

When the time came for Rachael, the eldest grandchild, to open her first box, she smiled and ripped into the paper. There, beneath the holiday wrap, was a beautiful picture of a violin—right on the front of the decorative cardboard box my mother had purchased earlier that year. Now, this particular granddaughter was studying the violin, both in school and in private lessons. She was so impressed that her gift was in a violin box that we didn't have the heart to tell her it had just happened that way.

After all the gifts were shared and cleanup had begun, we decided to keep the boxes at Grandma's for next year's use.

When the following Christmas rolled around and it came time to open the gifts, the entire family assembled on the porch again. The sitting places were a bit tighter, as the children were another year older. A shout of joy went up as one of the children ripped open the wrapping paper and found the violin box again. This year it held a Christmas outfit from Grandma.

Each year after that, the children looked at the wrapped presents, sizing each up and wondering who would end up with the special violin box. And as is the way with traditions, the excitement of knowing the violin box would be beneath the tree grew into a special memory.

As the years passed, however, that dear old box began to wear and tear. I patched it with tape and added staples, but as the years raced by, it finally happened. One year after Christmas, I was forced to decide. The violin box would no longer hold up under the duress of the season. It was a sad day when I placed it into the trash barrel. That box—just a cardboard box with the picture of a violin on the top—had been a precious and memorable part of our celebration.

A year or two passed. From time to time, we smiled and remembered the special little ritual we had enjoyed each Christmas with a box embossed with the picture of a violin. The next year, we picked up a new package of wrapping boxes. What a joy to open the package and to find in its center a violin box just like the one that had served us so well for so long!

That year, we purposefully used the new violin box to wrap a gift for the oldest granddaughter, now an adult. As our family gathered in our traditional spot on the porch and sat around the tree, Rachael opened her gift and her eyes lit in remembrance.

"I have the violin box!" she shouted.

That simple box reinforced our family's memories and traditions. It proved to us once again that it doesn't take much to create a personal and special atmosphere around those you love, as long as you share in that love.

As I watched the happy faces around the tree that year, I was reminded that although people pass from our lives there is nothing that can remove the memories of the people we hold dear. It is those very memories and traditions that will continue to be passed down from generation to generation to become the legacy that we—like the tattered old violin box—will eventually leave behind.

> *"Before you begin your Christmas meal, go around the dinner table and give each diner the opportunity to talk about what Christmas means to him or her."*

BY SONJA HERBERT

𝔏etting the 𝔏ight 𝔖hine

B y the end of November, my parents, Mutti and Vati, had efficiently packed our family into a caravan as snuggly as Vati, the owner of our little carnival, had packed the merry-go-round and the shooting hall into each other. It was a welcome respite. Our parents no longer had to work weekends, which meant we could all be together even on Sundays.

It was the winter of my fourteenth year, and the last Sunday in November was even more special to me. Like a comforting blanket, expectation hung thick in the warm air of our small caravan home, as we six children helped Mutti fashion an Advent wreath from fir boughs. As Mutti baked the traditional batch of sugar cookies for our Advent celebration, the vanilla fragrance mingled with the piney scent of our wreath and drifted from the kitchen compartment.

"Can I taste one of the cookies?" Franz, my ten-year-old brother called hopefully from the living room.

"You know perfectly well they are for after the Advent celebration," Mutti declared, without looking up.

Franz grumbled and returned to cutting out a wooden picture with his coping saw.

Nearby, seven-year-old Eva sat on the bus seat Vati had fastened to the floor, in front of the table for a kitchen bench, and looked at a piece of paper in her hand. "Look what I'm doing for the First Advent," she said, smiling in satisfaction as she held up a picture of a Christmas tree with a doll sitting primly beneath it.

I looked at the picture and shrugged. "It will be hard to see when only one candle is lit."

Unconcerned, Eva placed the picture on the table before her. "That's okay," she replied. "I'll describe it to everybody."

Mutti glanced at me sharply and frowned. "Leave the child alone," she said, as she placed the last of the cookies on a plate. "It's all right to do something different." For a moment, the expression on her face softened, as if she was thinking of something else. She sighed softly and then turned back to me. "What are *you* going to do for First Advent?"

"I'm not sure yet," I answered, though I had already decided. I wanted it to be a surprise. I knew Advent was much more than the beginning of wishing for toys and thinking of presents—as it always was in our family—and I wanted my parents and siblings to know that, too.

Earlier this fall, I had met two American evangelists at a free English course my sisters and I had attended. They confirmed my secret belief in Christ and invited me to visit their church. Though Mutti did not talk about Jesus, I thought she still believed in Him, because she allowed me to attend. Surely, she knew I would learn great and important news about Christ. Still, since my parents never acted as though Jesus was important, I wasn't sure how my family would feel about my First Advent offering.

Finally, dusk descended. After a hastily eaten supper of cheese and liverwurst sandwiches, Vati gathered the family for the traditional lighting of the Advent wreath. "It's time to celebrate the First Advent," he announced.

Little Michael squeezed past me and toddled into the living room. I sat on the sofa next to Carmen, who at sixteen was the oldest.

Mutti and Vati sat opposite us in their easy chairs. Michael, on Vati's lap, stared with big eyes at the coffee table, which held the Christmas wreath with the candles still unlit.

The yearly ritual began as Mutti rose ceremoniously. "Once again the Christmas season has begun," she said softly. "In four weeks and two days Christmas will be here, and the Advent candles will light our way to Santa Claus and our presents."

I watched in fascination as Mutti turned off the electric lights, took a box of matches from the table, and lit the first of the Advent candles. Next Sunday there would be two, then three, and on the last Sunday before Christmas all four of the candles would brighten our small home.

"I've had my say, and now it's your turn," Mutti said, turning to her eldest child. "Carmen, you start."

Carmen rose and recited a poem about a lonely fir tree in the woods that wanted to be a Christmas tree. Then it was my turn. I stood. Suddenly, I wished I had thought of something else. Knowing I had no choice but to continue, I cleared my dry throat and began.

"Christmas is not just about presents," I whispered, as I looked from one member of my family to the next. "It's about Jesus. Advent means *the Coming*. Today's candle represents the prophets' first words about Him, long before He was born. Next week, we light two candles and that means we know even more about Christ. On the third Sunday, three candles will give our caravan more light—like the way the world turned brighter right before Jesus came. On the last Advent, the darkness is almost gone, and then on Christmas Day, the tree glows with many candles to show Jesus is the light of the world."

As I sat down, Mutti nodded. "That was interesting," she said, "but let's not get too religious, child. You want to have some fun in life, too." Then she abruptly turned toward little Josefa and smiled. "Your turn now."

My face turned bright red as my younger sister stood, her eyes fixed on the candle, and told the story about a poor little girl who had to sell matches on Christmas Eve. Josefa was a good storyteller, but I wasn't listening. While I had talked about Jesus, I had seen Carmen grin. She had been amused by my story, and Mutti had worried that I was being too religious. Though my face burned in embarrassment, I knew I had to follow my conviction. And deep in my heart I knew I had explained something important to my family, even if they weren't ready to accept it. I vowed that one day my own children would learn the story of Jesus and the lighting of the Advent wreath would be as special to my children as it had been to me when I was a child.

It would be years later before I understood why my mother never talked about Jesus. She had escaped the Holocaust by obtaining employment in the circus, but she had also lost her faith in a loving God. Even though she didn't believe in Jesus, she wanted her children to experience the same holiday magic other children did, and she accomplished this in her very own way.

Eventually, I moved to the United States. When I had children of my own, we celebrated our own version of Advent. As it had been for me and my siblings, my children, too, looked forward to the magic of the wreath, the sugar cookies, the lighting of the candles, and theirs and their siblings' presentations. But in our family our presentations always centered on the most important gift, the wonderful present God gave us: His Son.

"When it comes to the magic of Christmas gifts, always try to give something your children haven't asked for and don't expect but will never forget."

BY NANCY ALLAN

The Thank-You Kiss

My Christmas memories are as fragile as the silver-glass spire that reigned over our Christmas tree each year. It was the same spire that had brightened the Christmases of my father, his siblings, his mother, and her brother and sister.

This magical spire was so delicate that each year it was kept in a soft hand-knit stocking, until it was taken out for its command performance. My father swore it was the stocking Grandmother had knit for his grandfather. The matching hat—sturdy and a little worse for wear—was a big part of our Christmas memories.

My sister and I were the youngest of four children. Though we were raised during the Depression, somehow our parents always seemed to manage wonderful Christmases for us. I often look back, and even though the memories are slippery with age, I wonder at the magic of it all.

Our tree always seemed bigger than everyone else's. The paper angels, with their painted cheeks and marcelled hair, were lovely. As a child, I believed with all my heart that they were real angels sent down from heaven to be with our family for the most special time of the year. The glass birds, with their stiff brush tails, glistened and made us proud to have such a beautiful species on our tree. We had bells and balls of every color, and tinsel that glittered and shone from every branch. It amazes me that while I can recall all of the wonderful treasures that we decorated our Christmas tree with, I do not have a clue as to whether or not we had lights on the tree.

Of course, I remember the traditional baking, the quick hiding of packages, the air of secrecy that spread through the house as the big day grew closer, and how the Christmas cards would begin arriving.

My sister Jean and I marveled at each card left by the postman. Mail itself was exciting, but to receive such beautiful cards with lines of flowing poetry inside was delicious reading. Jean and I read and reread those cards. After a while, we invented a game simply called *The Christmas Card Game*.

As the Christmas cards began to pile up on our buffet in the dining room, the fun began. Jean, being three years older than me, started the game. She instructed me to sit on the floor in the living room and wait while she put the cards into an old soup kettle. Then, one at a time, she would hold up a card for me to see. It might have a picture of holly, or Santa with one foot down the chimney, or flying reindeer, or the stable with the new baby, adoring shepherds, and the Magi.

"Now," she said, "remember the picture, and then you must remember who sent it."

"Merry Christmas from the Bradleys," I cried, as I looked at a picture of Santa stockings hung by a chimney. For the next card, I shouted, "Love to all from Bob and Eileen!"

For weeks before Christmas, we played our carefree game. There were many, many cards, but by the time Christmas came, we were almost card-perfect.

Even our older brother and sister seemed to get a kick out of watching us play. Once my brother, Bill, said, "Hey, can I play?" He snatched a card from us and pretended to read it.

"Merry Christmas to two homely girls," he crowed. Then he ran around the room, waving the card. We immediately screamed to Mother.

"Find something constructive to do!" Mother yelled from the kitchen. Bill made his most ferocious face, obediently put on his jacket, and went outside to throw snowballs at the garage.

One year, as we played our Christmas card game, we were oblivious to the fact that something was amiss. Apparently, Mother had found two beautiful bathrobes for my sister and me and put them in layaway. Each week, she had paid a little something on them, so they would be paid in full by Christmas. Though my mother was an excellent seamstress, and we always had very nice clothes, she had wanted us to have something that was bought at a store. This was to be her triumph. But someone threw a monkey wrench in the works when he forgot to pick up the layaway before the store closed on Christmas Eve.

There was much muffled yelling, and then Bill went down to the basement with tears on his face. My sister and I were quite absorbed in playing the Christmas card game and didn't pay much attention. We did, however, hear my mother on the telephone.

"I know it's Christmas Eve for you, too," she said apologetically. "But . . . this is very important."

I suppose the beauty of a small town is that everyone knows everyone else, and my mother knew the manager of the Montgomery Ward store that held our robes captive.

Not too much later, Mother slipped her coat on and went outside. Almost immediately, an old black car drove up, and a man got out and handed her a large package. When my mother took the package from him, she quickly leaned over and kissed him on the cheek.

We preened in front of the mirror the next morning in our gorgeous new robes. We didn't take them off until it was time to go to Mass. Sometimes, I wondered if I had dreamed I saw mother kissing the Montgomery Ward manager. But when I grew up and married, and started a family of my own, I realized what I had seen that night had been a thank-you kiss. My mother, a very grateful woman, had thanked the manager of that store for helping her to keep her children's Christmas magical in the only way she could—a kiss on the cheek. I imagine she also told him he was an angel, or a dear, for helping—that part I will never know, but I can imagine.

As with all Christmas stories, this story has been retold over and over and become a family favorite. Now my children repeat it to their children. It isn't easy for them to understand about putting robes on layaway and having the store manager deliver the garments. But they do understand taking out Christmas memories, dusting them off, and hanging them in our hearts to cherish for all time.

"Take a favorite pastime and give it a special spin. Take the kids sledding at midnight on Christmas Eve!"

BY CAROL MCADOO REHME

Moon Flight

"Kyle, Katrina," I whispered from the foot of the ladder leading to the loft. "Kayla, Koy." I raised my voice a bit louder. "Kids, wake up."

Someone mumbled and snuggled deeper into a cozy cot.

"Kids, it's nearly midnight. The moon is out. Get up!"

"The moon!" Excited whispers mingled with giggles and yawns.

I grinned to know their eyes had opened wide. I heard them toss back toasty quilts and groan when their feet touched the frigid floor. Searching with flashlights, they fumbled for clothes stacked ready on the shelf. Over long underwear, they knew to add thick socks, woolen sweaters, and denim pants. With quick steps, they flew down the ladder and followed the glow of the small lantern hanging by the cabin door. They pulled hooded coats, heavy boots, and fleecy mittens from the hooks—eager for our annual midnight ride. But tonight's adventure would be a ride of a different color.

Bundled up tight, they finally gathered outside. Together, we loosened the rope handles hitched to the railing of the porch. As in years past, no one said a word, awed by the mystery of this unique family tradition.

Thud. Four red sleds plopped to the ground.

Crunch. Six pairs of boots broke the crusted snow.

Swish. The whispering sleds coasted behind us like hushed travelers on a silent night.

Suddenly, I stopped and pointed. "There it is, kids," I breathed. "Just like I promised. This year we have a blue moon for the Christmas holidays!"

The fat-faced moon hung high.

"Blue moon? Aw, Mom, it's the same old white moon. It isn't blue at all," said Koy, our budding scientist.

"Well, no, it's not," I agreed, "but see how round and shiny it is?"

He rolled his eyes. "Of course. That's because it's a full moon."

"Ah, but not just any full moon. It's the second full moon this month. That makes it a blue moon."

"Oh, I get it." Koy's eyes widened with renewed interest. "Blue moon is only a name."

"That's right," I said, "but look around you. Doesn't everything *seem* blue?"

It was true. Bluish moonbeams, as bright as streetlights, flooded the meadow. Naked tree branches cast lacy night-shadows on the glowing ground. And the new snow glistened like diamond dust.

"Wow! The moon is so bright, I can see everything!" Kayla's whisper puffed out in silvery clouds.

My husband slipped his arms around their shoulders. "A blue moon is rare. So rare, it appears only once every few years." He gazed up at the huge orb. "And this one belongs exclusively to the six of us!"

With my own heart thumping at the novelty of the night, I stood still and breathed the sharp cold air. I gazed at the pearly polished hill stretching down to the steep lane. Then I glanced over my shoulder.

The mountain cabin was a gingerbread house dripping with frosting. Our fresh footprints made a freckled path winding from its porch, with the sled tracks a long trail of slender holiday ribbons.

A crisp night. A fresh snow. And a brand-new moon.

Katrina rubbed her eyes and whispered, "This feels like a dream . . . a fairytale dream."

My gloved hand squeezed hers. "Well, what are we waiting for? It's time to celebrate. Let's slide!"

Crunch! Swish! The kids pulled their wooden sleds toward the crest of the snow-packed lane.

"Here I go!" Kyle shouted as he raced ahead, belly-flopped onto his sled, and sailed off. On its downward path, the metal runners scraped bits of gravel, first on one side, then the other. And each time they did, tiny star-bursts shot out like sparklers on the Fourth of July.

At the bottom of the hill, Kyle slid to a stop.

"You're next, Katrina!" he shouted across the crisp air to the top of the hilly road.

Kayla waited while Katrina positioned her sled.

"Ready, set, go!" She gave her sister a push and watched her glide away.

Katrina's sled dipped down, up, and down again, with the momentum of a roller coaster. Runner sparks twinkled under the blue moon as she flew to the bottom of the slope.

My husband and Koy squeezed onto his smaller sled, and we watched them trail Katrina like the vapor of a comet's tail.

Then Kayla scooted her own sled into place. Sitting down, she wiggled to the front and braced her heels against the V-shaped metal frame.

I sat behind her, my arms tight around her waist. She looped the rope around her wrist and leaned to one side. Her mittened hand shoved hard against the icy ground.

Once. Twice. Three times. The sled inched forward and quickly gathered speed on the steep slope. Fast. And faster. The sled skimmed across the diamond-studded lane and downward. Kayla's bangs blew straight up. She held the rope tight.

Plink. The runners scraped small stones. My eyes watered in the rush of the wind. She steered us to the right.

Whoosh, whoosh. The sled started to slow. My nose numb, I stared up at the moon-bright sky and at the shadows painting the ground.

Our sled slowed to a stop.

Giggling, Kayla somersaulted into a mound of white while I stood. She pillowed her head in the fluffy snow bed and flapped her arms in the loose powder to etch a snow angel.

Smiling up at me she begged. "Please, oh, please! Can we do it again?"

"Why not?" I agreed. "After all, tonight is ours." I spread my arms wide to hug the sky. "And a Christmas night like this happens only once—once in a blue moon!"

> *"Quality family time is time spent together doing something everyone enjoys. For a new twist on an old favorite, let each member of the family select a day from the song 'The Twelve Days of Christmas' and then change the words to suit your family."*

BY SHEILA O'BRIEN SCHIMPF

Wired

T he first Christmas our son was away from home, he wasn't just away from home. He had a job on a Pacific island near the equator, almost 9,000 miles from his family! That year my sister also opted to keep her family of four home in Minneapolis, and my brother stayed with his family in Baltimore.

Home in Michigan, we felt the responsibility of continuing traditions—a freshly cut tree, ornaments from four decades, presents, stockings, and the family Christmas dinner consisting of prime rib and homemade cookies. We had dinner for seven: my parents and my sister, our two adult children, my husband, and me.

But no matter how we figured it, we did not see how we could manage Christmas without singing "The Twelve Days of Christmas." Our family tradition, corny and fun, had started when my generation married and had children. At that point, our family had grown to twelve around the dinner table. The following year, when I realized we were all looking forward to singing that silly nonsense song again, I knew a tradition had been born.

"The Twelve Days of Christmas" is a cumulative song. It starts with one verse, then that verse is repeated, and another is added. Both are repeated and a third is added. The song continues for twelve verses. It requires a few memory tricks, a little nerve, a lot of give–and-take, and a willingness to take turns. In short, it takes the same skills required to survive in a family.

After Christmas dinner, when everyone was filled with good food, we each picked a day. Usually the youngest got to be the first day of Christmas, because he relished singing "a partridge and a pear tree" twelve times. We hammed it up—"five gooooooooolden rings"—and laughed more than we sang. If someone lost track of maids and geese and hens and lords and inserted the wrong group in a verse, we laughed even harder.

When my mother found a set of twelve china bells, each labeled with one of the twelve days, we added nonstop bell ringing to our manic rendition. The bells took their place on the table, right beside the candles, the good dishes, and Grandmother's silver spoons.

Singing the song with only seven in Michigan that year just wouldn't be the same. We needed the squeaky high voices, the deep rolling voices, the loud booming voices, the shy uncomfortable voices. We needed all the familiar voices we had grown up with, voices we knew singing Happy Birthday, Irish lullabies, college fight songs, and "The Star Spangled Banner." Those voices were the tones and vibrations imprinted on our hearts.

We simply had to have everyone's voice or it wouldn't feel like Christmas.

With that thought, the tech generation went to work. It was Christmas, after all, and miracles have been known to happen. Our small miracle required belief in the global village and an adroitness with technology. By appointment, our son in Palau called us on our computer with iChat software. No extra cost. We used cell phones to call our sister in Minneapolis and our brother in Baltimore. The two cells set to "speaker phone" lay on the table near the computer speakers. We could hear everybody. They could hear everybody.

Within minutes, we had connected fourteen people; there were my husband and I, our two grown children, my parents and sister in Michigan; our son in Palau; my sister, her husband, and their two children in Minneapolis, and my brother and his wife in Baltimore. Because we now had more than the song required, my brother, his wife, and my father all agreed to share a day.

It worked!

Each person added a verse—loud and clear—and we all chimed in on the chorus. In between we heard the laughter.

A three-second time-lag from Palau meant Tim was the last one to finish every verse. His voice coming to us loud and clear from 9,000 miles away was calm and steady, but my heart was pumping wildly. It was exhilarating to beat the sadness I felt when I realized we couldn't be together at Christmas.

We made it through all twelve days, one at a time, and then together we sang the whole song again as a group, just as we do when we're sitting around the holiday table, candles burning, pushing cookie crumbs back and forth on the tablecloth next to tea mugs.

It was a brilliant Christmas moment, etched forever in the Christmas memory bank of the five in the youngest generation. It symbolized who we are—slightly crazy, creative people with a genetic sense of humor, and a willingness to make time for family. This is what we do every Christmas, in person or by taking advantage of twenty-first century technology. And this is what we will continue to do, because for this family, being together is what it's all about.

> *"On Christmas Eve each year, play a certain album or CD that reminds you of the songs your mother used to listen to on Christmas Eve when you were a child."*

BY PATRICIA F. D'ASCOLI

The Best Christmas Ever

My mother's soul was filled with music, and so was our home. If she wasn't playing her piano, then the sound of music was coming from the old record player. Listening to and absorbing the wonderful classical music selections that Mother played was a joyous part of my childhood. Our mutual love of music was a special bond between us.

One of the most memorable recordings my mother owned was a collection of Christmas songs called *The Heart of Christmas*, sung by Sergio Franchi, an Italian tenor, who was one of her favorite singers. She bought his Christmas album in 1967, when I was four years old, and played it every single Christmas when I was growing up. This album became not only a symbol of Christmas for me, but also a symbol of my mother.

After I got married and moved into my own home in the same town, I always returned to my mother's home at Christmas to hear the familiar songs of my childhood. Even though the record was beginning to wear and was scratchy in places, we loved to sing the words of "Buon Natale," an upbeat and happy Italian Christmas song. When I married my husband, Raphael, who also is Italian, the words suddenly seemed prophetic. Before long, it became one of my husband's favorite songs, too.

A few years later, totally out of the blue, my mother and stepfather announced they were selling their house and moving to a condominium across the state. Even though I was twenty-five and a grown married woman, I took the news poorly. I enjoyed dropping in on my mother frequently or meeting for lunch in town. I didn't want her to live two hours away. I tried to be brave but was deeply saddened when she moved.

I missed Mother terribly. As childish as it may seem, I felt as if she had abandoned me. Even when she invited us over for Thanksgiving in her new home, which of course was filled with the sound of her familiar music, it still made me sad to think I could not access this connection with her the way I had before. And with Christmas approaching, I dreaded the thought of spending the holidays apart, separated by more than a hundred miles.

As the Christmas season began, I worried that things would never be the same. I kept remembering how we had always gone Christmas shopping, decorated her tree, and wrapped presents together, and I longed for it to be the same this year.

Christmas morning arrived in all its glory with a fine dusting of snow and a chill in the air. My tree was decorated beautifully with special ornaments and twinkled with little colored lights. Presents peeped out expectantly from under the fragrant tree, where my husband and I had placed them the night before. Our stockings, filled with surprises, and Christmas cards from friends and relatives, were displayed throughout the living room. But something was missing.

Christmas is not a time for tears, but I felt like crying. My husband was a wonderful, kind, and loving man. I had a good life, a great job, and a future career as an attorney. *This will pass*, I told myself, as Raphael and I sat down with our coffee and began to exchange gifts.

Raphael, ever the thoughtful gift buyer, had selected a lovely blouse, a robe, and other items for me, all of which were perfect. He was thrilled as well by the presents I'd purchased for him. Soon the room was filled with discarded green-and-red paper, and gold ribbons snaked their way around the floor, where our cat happily pounced on them, shredding them to bits. Our gift exchange had been a success, but as I prepared to shower and dress for our visit to his parents' house, sadness crept over me. Perhaps Raphael noticed for he stopped and peered into my eyes.

"There's one more present I want to give you," he said, before he disappeared down the hallway that led to our bedroom. When he returned, he was carrying a thin square package wrapped in shiny gold paper.

Gingerly, I ripped the paper back to expose a record album that was so familiar I had to fight back tears. The smiling picture of Sergio Franchi on the cover brought all my past Christmases to mind and my heart overflowed with love for the man I had married, who apparently knew me so well.

It was *The Heart of Christmas*, circa 1965. Raphael had found it in an obscure little record shop in New York City that specialized in out-of-print albums. On the back, in my husband's bold hand, were the words *"Buon Natale, Mi Amore."*

I dashed to the turntable and carefully placed my treasured recording on the spindle, watching anxiously as the needle touched the ancient vinyl. Soon the strains of "Buon Natale" rang out from the speakers like an old friend calling my name and wishing me Merry Christmas. And it was a merry Christmas. As Raphael took me in his arms, I suddenly saw this Christmas for what it was—the best Christmas ever!

> *"Make an annual holiday pilgrimage to the local Goodwill, or Salvation Army center, to donate the toys your children have outgrown."*

BY GEORGIA A. HUBLEY

Two Christmas Wishes

When I was six years old, my Christmas wish was that a doll with porcelain skin would be sitting under the tree on Christmas morning. I wanted my doll to have eyelashes, eyes that opened and closed, and long brown hair that I could comb.

I had a small brown chenille teddy bear I called Teddy and a rag doll with yellow-yarn braids named Joy. Both were special to me, but both were tattered and worn. Mom was an excellent seamstress and did the best she could to keep them repaired, but stuffing peeped out of their seams from time to time.

Late one night, a week before Christmas, when I was supposed to be sound asleep, I overheard Mom and Dad talking about money being scarce and a wave of disappointment washed over me.

"There aren't many spare dollars for Christmas in the cookie jar," Dad said.

"Not to worry," Mom replied, "I'm going to the church rummage sale tomorrow. Maybe I'll find some bargains."

I choked back the tears. I didn't want my folks to know I'd eavesdropped, or how sad I felt about not getting a new doll for Christmas. I hugged and kissed Teddy and Joy. "I love you both," I whispered.

After lunch on Christmas Eve, Mom asked my younger brother and me to help decorate sugar cookies. We were enthralled by the many preparations underway: the delicious aromas coming from the kitchen; wrapping paper, ribbons, and bows strewn all over the dining room table; and the continuous reverberation of Mom's sewing machine as she finished making last-minute gifts for everyone on her list.

"I can hardly wait until Christmas morning," my brother confided, as he pushed a gumdrop onto a newly frosted cookie. "I wished for a new sled."

My chest tightened. I looked into his happy face and tried to smile back. I just couldn't tell him he probably wouldn't be getting a sled.

"I wished for a new doll," I said quietly.

When Mom and Dad tucked us into bed that night, they were exuberant. Suddenly I, too, felt happy and was eager for Christmas morning to arrive. I hugged Teddy and Joy tightly. I didn't need a new doll.

I will never forget that Christmas morning in 1945. My brother ran downstairs ahead of me. I was stunned when he shouted, "I see a red sled under the tree!"

My eyes welled with tears of joy when I spotted the most beautiful doll waiting for me. It was love at first sight. I named her Rita. She was a very old doll and had been someone else's treasure, but she was brand-new to me. Rita had long auburn hair, a porcelain face, and a white muslin body, and her eyes opened and closed. She even had eyelashes! What's more, Rita's dress matched the red-and-white paisley print dress Mom had made me for Christmas.

What a joyous and festive Christmas we had with family and friends—a day topped off by the delicious feast Mom prepared. Even though bedtime was later than usual on Christmas, I couldn't fall asleep after being tucked in. Quietly, I got out of bed and tiptoed to the top of the stairs to listen to the murmuring voices I heard below.

"I'm sure obliged to the hardware store owner and his son for restoring old sleds and selling them at a fair price," Dad said.

"And I am so grateful for the dolls donated to the rummage sale," Mom replied.

The following November, after the first snowfall, my brother and I went sledding down the big hill behind our farmhouse. Much to my brother's dismay, he barely fit on his sled. That evening, he added a sled to the top of his Christmas list. On Christmas morning, he found a larger sled under the tree. After that Christmas, a tradition began; Dad and my brother donated all of his outgrown sleds for restoration.

As for me, I placed Rita under the tree on Christmas Eve, and for many Christmas mornings that followed, I found her right where I had left her, and she was always wearing a brand-new outfit. To make my Christmas complete, there was always a matching outfit for me, too!

> *"Trade in the hustle and bustle of department store shopping for the simple easy lifestyle you grew up with. This year, go back to basics and exchange homemade gifts."*

BY M. DELORIS HENSCHEID

Macaroni Necklaces and Cumbersome Pride

Teaching our older children to make Christmas gifts for one another started as a simple, fun activity. Making the gifts kept their little hands busy and their growing minds creatively engaged. However, by the time our brood expanded to nine, manufacturing eighty-one gifts would have become a logistical nightmare—had we not introduced the magic of drawing names.

The first exciting drawing took place on Thanksgiving many years ago. Over the following weeks, with clenched lips, the little ones kneaded homemade play dough, placing it in small jars with tight lids. They scribbled pictures, made blocks of wood or spools into dolls, ruled crooked lines onto sheets of paper for stationery, and dyed macaroni and strung it on yarn for exotic necklaces. Over the years, projects took more time and gifts became works of art, but always one or two macaroni necklaces were made on the sly.

By 1971, the children had matured from nineteen years down to seven, and our eldest had left for college. About that time, a chronic kidney disorder I had been plagued with worsened and several surgeries followed. Two of our daughters were found to have inherited the same condition and both underwent surgery. My husband's business suffered because of his absence and on a rainy September afternoon, he collapsed. He was diagnosed with hypertension and clinical depression and was hospitalized as well.

The older children at home, all with after-school jobs, did the best they could to hold the reins, while relatives and friends helped when possible.

Somehow, we all managed to be home for Thanksgiving. After dinner the children asked, "Mom, do you have the names to draw?"

Draw names? I hadn't even given it a thought. Thankfully, someone ran to get paper and pencil. One by one the children drew out one slip of paper and then whispered the name that was written on it into my ear.

That evening my husband returned to the hospital, but during the following month he found comfort, healing, and his future profession, while making Christmas gifts in the woodshop. The therapist suggested he fashion small rectangle boxes, wish all his troubles into them, and then glue on the top. That year each of his five daughters received a lovely handmade jewelry box for Christmas.

During those same weeks, while sitting by our little girls' hospital beds, I embroidered different colored kittens on pillowcases. At home, I sewed Nehru shirts (the fashion of the day) for the boys. As I worked on a flannel nightgown for our oldest daughter, I noticed the boys disappear to the garage, basement, or their rooms often to work on their gifts. And when she had a free moment, their big sister's knitting needles flew!

As down as our circumstances appeared—and often felt—we were at least somewhat grounded because we were engaged in the familiar project of making something for someone we loved. Our little tradition, the strongest thread of our fragile existence, was helping mend our hearts, bodies, and minds as we looked forward to a new and better year.

It was during the first week of December, just after we had pulled up our proverbial bootstraps, when an acquaintance who was a member of a local woman's association called to let me know we had been chosen the family of the year.

"DeLoris," she said, "it has been brought to the attention of the Christmas Project members that your family is having a difficult time this year, and we'd like to help."

"Help *us*?" I asked in mock confusion. "Oh, thank you, but we're doing just fine. I'm sure you can find a family who really needs some help."

"I hope you will think this over," the lady continued.

After I hung up, I sat at the table stirring a cup of coffee, muttering and arguing with myself. *Dear God, us? Needy? What had we done to become the needy family of the year?*

The next afternoon the doorbell rang. I was shocked when I opened the door to find the Christmas Project lady.

"I'm sorry to bother you," she said, "but I thought it might help if I came and explained just what we had in mind and, I hope, put your mind at ease."

After we talked, I finally agreed but decided to keep the project to myself.

The weekend before Christmas the children decorated the traditional cedar tree brought in from the hills and, one by one, their wrapped gifts appeared beneath it.

On Christmas Eve morning, boxes with bright packages, the makings for Christmas dinner, even a small television, appeared at the door. The children went wild with excitement and curiosity.

"Where did all this stuff come from, Mom?" they shouted excitedly.

I shrugged my shoulders. "Santa must have a lot of leftovers this year."

Later that night, when the younger children were tucked into bed, the older children demanded a straight answer. The eldest looked me straight in the eye.

"What gives, Mom?"

They deserved an answer, so I explained. Then I asked them to accept the fact that we have generous friends and leave it at that. They quietly nodded their heads and went off to bed.

The next morning, as the younger children opened their mystery gifts, the older children oohed and awed as if nothing unusual was happening. Then they quickly scrambled into the circle for the most important tradition of the season and called out, beginning with the oldest, "All right, Henry, who did you get?" With each gift there were squeals, hugs, and even a few tears. The most treasured moment for me was counting the number of macaroni necklaces that appeared that year.

And even now, with children and grandchildren scattered from shore to shore, on occasion, a mysterious macaroni necklace appears in someone's Christmas box.

"Everyone changes. Over the course of a year, everything from facial features to size to clothing styles change. This year, ask each member of the family to sign a Christmas poster so you can see how their handwriting changes, too."

BY KEVIN LYNCH

The Autograph Collector

Compared to my mother's style of holiday decorating, my grandmother's struck me as a little quirky.

In our house, my mom dressed the table with a pricey set of holiday-themed table linens and adorned the mantel with florist-cut garlands and special candles. Grandmother decorated her table with commemorative jelly jars, and placed pipe-cleaner elves and glittered reindeer with beer-can bodies on her mantel. For a number of years, we hid our tree beneath mounds of tinsel, while Grandmother added glitter to her rooms by placing plastic cases containing uncirculated silver coins that my grandfather had collected around her house. This, I assumed, was her way of introducing a little sparkle to the setting, or maybe she believed the shiny coins represented good fortune, or wealth, or maybe they were meant to convey a patriotic sentiment.

One year, my grandmother pinned up a poster she had purchased in a stationer's shop. The drawing was of Tiny Tim perched on his dad's, Bob Cratchit's, shoulder. They were coming toward the viewer along a narrow old London street. The snow looked fresh and the gas lamps had orange halos. The caption at the bottom of the poster read, of course, "God bless us, every one!"

The Cratchit pinup made its first appearance next to the Christmas tree around the same time as about a dozen babies came into the world, by way of our family tree. Some of us in this happy drooling hoard were close enough in age that we possessed the urge—one shared by many toddlers—to write on the walls. One of my cousins, which one is lost in the mists of time, unthinkingly decided to make his or her mark on the new poster. My grandmother found this to be wonderful! In a fit of inspiration, she asked everyone present that Christmas to sign their name. The following Christmases she rehung the poster and again asked for autographs.

After five or six years, the portrait of Tiny Tim and his father was cluttered with names. It took until the end of the decade before we realized what we had hanging before us. A family time capsule, of sorts, that we lightheartedly examined once a year rather than a century later.

Reading the names on the poster, we could trace the changes in our family and in ourselves. By singling out a child's name—which first appeared as a tentative scribble with a backward letter, then changed into a more legible name with the symbol of a heart instead of a dot above the letter i, continuing on until the signature was the hurried scrawl of a late teen—we could chart his or her development. New names appeared on the posters, those of my aunts and uncles, and of various boyfriends and girlfriends. Sometimes those names remained when the young couple became man and wife. Other times, they vanished, the result of a breakup. Entire love lives could be charted on the poster.

Names, like Uncle Tim's, ceased to appear for other reasons. Though he was no longer with us on Christmas, his presence remained in the form of his signature. It reminded us of better times, times when he had his health. Sometimes names did not appear because an uncle in the service had been stationed far away over the holidays, or because a recently married relation was having Christmas with new in-laws.

In its way, the poster became a friendly version of *The Ghost of Christmas Past*. Like the Dickensian spirit, the graffiti-covered image could take us by the hand and lead us to a different place in time. Tracing the evolution of a signature reminded us of who we had once been and what we had become. Certain signatures reminded us of particular holidays and invariably prompted someone to remark, "That was the year Uncle George sat down and broke the chair," or "That was the Christmas all the kids ate too much turkey then fell asleep in a big heap in front of the fireplace."

Looking back, it now seems obvious that my grandmother understood what she had started so long ago, when she requested each of our signatures on her mildly kitschy poster. Now, in our house in her memory we hang a similar poster and those who gather with us to celebrate the holidays are asked to sign their name, too. For me, the simple act of scanning the names on our Christmas poster brings those people back to me. It also makes me realize—among so many other things—that my grandmother's *seemingly* quirky decorating style was really the best.

"Start a holiday book tradition with your children or grandchildren. The book can be about anything at all, but try to incorporate some aspect of the book into your life."

BY RUTH COE CHAMBERS

Of Books and Dogs and Dreams Coming True

From the time our children were toddlers, we included a book in each of their stockings. Nothing was more fun than shopping for just the right book for each of our girls. One Christmas the innocent purchase of a small paperback by Albert Payson Terhune titled *Lad: A Dog* turned our lives upside down.

The story—in print since 1919—is about a remarkable collie. When I slipped the book into our eight-year-old daughter's Christmas stocking, I never dreamed it would set us off on such an enduring odyssey.

Completely enthralled by the book, Megan lay down beside the tree—leaving unopened Christmas gifts for later—while she read Terhune's masterpiece. We had never seen anything like it. *What child leaves Christmas gifts unopened?* Later, Megan sat in front of a roaring fire, still reading. In fact, the closed book was on her lap during Christmas dinner and in the pocket of her new flannel nightgown at bedtime!

At the breakfast table the next morning, Megan placed the book on the table and announced, "I want a collie pup."

Hot coffee flew out of my mouth. We already had three dogs! A frown crossed my face as I looked at her. "Aren't Serenade, Smithy, and Sadie enough?" I asked.

"We don't have a collie," she replied, as though that settled the matter.

I rolled my eyes heavenward. "No, but we have a sheltie, a cairn terrier, and a mutt."

Undeterred, on every holiday that year Megan asked for a collie pup—including April Fool's Day! And on Christmas the following year, she used her allowance to buy a wicker dog bed and red plaid mattress as a hint for Santa. She left it under the tree with a note, along with cookies and milk on the hearth for Santa. Sure enough, the next morning a small dog was asleep in the bed.

Unfortunately, it was the wrong dog.

"Sadie," Megan shouted at the poor startled canine. "Look what you've done!" Sadie, a small black dog of questionable ancestry, was smart and sweet and had been completely devoted to our family for years. Unfortunately, Megan was so smitten with the idea of a collie pup, she didn't consider anything else. Instead, she sobbed hysterically. "If Sadie hadn't slept in my puppy's bed, Santa would have left a collie pup!"

I wiped her tears and hugged her. "You can't know that, honey."

She raised confused tear-swollen eyes to me. Her voice shook as she spoke. "You've always said Christmas was a time of miracles. I thought a puppy would be my miracle."

I smoothed back her hair gently and smiled. "Maybe Sadie thought the bed was *her* Christmas miracle."

Megan sniffled. She cast a sidelong glance at Sadie. "I didn't think of that." She sniffed again as more tears cascaded down her face. "Poor Sadie."

Seeing my opportunity to change this sad morning into a happy one, I guided Megan toward the dog bed. "You could let her miracle come true, you know. She seems really attached to that bed."

Sadie wagged her tail hopefully as Megan knelt and hugged her. "Okay, you can have it," she said gruffly. "But only because it's Christmas."

My husband and I exchanged a look. How could we right this wrong for our little girl? We didn't get a collie that year, but while Megan began a collection of glass dogs and photographs—all collies, of course—my husband and I haunted used bookstores searching for more books by Terhune. Desperate to avoid bringing another dog into our home, we hoped to placate Megan, at least for a while longer. For her ninth birthday we flew to Sunnybank, the Terhune estate overlooks Pompton Lake in New Jersey, both as a family vacation and as a chance for Megan to further her study of Terhune.

Sunnybank, once the special Eden of the Terhune family, was a memorial park that housed Lad's grave. When Megan found the grave, she knelt and cried.

She turned to me and whispered with a shaky voice, "I read in one of my books that a lock of Lad's hair is in an envelope at the Library of Congress."

Megan wasn't the only one moved by that bit of information. My husband and I exchanged a look of pure compassion for our little girl and for the spirit of a dog that had long been absent from this earth but continued to touch so many lives.

In that moment, we learned a very big lesson as parents. We remembered the ease in which we'd purchased the book and understood there was no such way to buy a child.

The following year, when Megan turned ten, we bought her a beautiful sable and white collie pup, just like the one she had been dreaming about. The gratitude and love on Megan's face matched the happy grin on that squirming puppy's face and brought tears of joy to mine.

"You can never be too busy to dress up your family and get a holiday photo taken with Santa."

BY REBECCA BURGENER

Pictures with Santa

"This is it! This is the dress!" I shouted, as I pulled the tiny item off the rack and showed it to my husband, Jeff.

I had been searching for weeks. Anna was too big for the infant-size Mrs. Claus dress that included fuzzy white booties and a Santa hat, but the long red dress with white fluff all along the bottom edge that I now held securely in my hand was perfect!

"She can wear white, or maybe red, stockings and her red dress shoes, and we can get a red bow for her hair," I gushed.

I smiled down at my precious Anna. It was her second Christmas. I wanted everything to be perfect for her. When postpartum blues blindsided me, shortly after her birth, Anna became my very reason for living.

Jeff smiled his agreement, and we turned our attention to the next blessing God had sent us. Allen was only a few months old. We wanted him dressed as a fat little elf for his first Christmas picture with Santa. No expense was too much. I'd live off noodles until the next payday, if that's what it took to dress him. I would have, too, but the costume we'd hoped for simply was nowhere to be found.

To make matters worse, this would be the first Christmas we wouldn't be able to get our Santa pictures taken on Jeff's birthday, because Jeff had to work that day. The next weekend was almost too late. Christmas would be right around the corner and there'd be no money left for presents. Tears stung the back of my eyes. We *had* to get these pictures taken.

The tradition had started when Jeff and I had been dating. His family always decorated the Christmas tree on December 15, which was his dad's birthday. Jeff wanted to start a similar tradition on his birthday, which was December 18. A family photo seemed the perfect choice.

"Would you go with me to get pictures taken with Santa Claus?" he had asked shyly.

I looked at him and shrugged. If that was how he wanted to spend his nineteenth birthday, who was I to argue? "Sure," I replied.

I thought about that conversation now, as we searched for the elusive elf costume. Jeff had been so excited about that photo! I wished that excitement would return. Instead, these days, he stressed about bills and the lack of Christmas presents. I thought if we could just get the family photos with Santa Claus taken as close to his birthday as possible it might bring back his smile. I wanted to wipe the worry away for good.

Since Allen already had the belly, we finally settled on a Santa Claus suit for him.

On picture day, we stood in line at the mall. While we waited, a former teacher walked through with his wife and stopped to say hello.

"I assume you're not working, since you have these guys," he said gently, referring to my children.

I raised my chin a notch and looked him square in the face. "I'm tutoring," I said without mentioning that I was doing so for free.

That particular teacher had witnessed me struggle through a degree that could have gotten me a job—a well-paying job. I couldn't help but think he thought I had thrown something away by choosing to be a stay-at-home mother instead. But I hadn't. At this moment in my life, I was doing what I needed to do. I was giving my attention to my children, the ones in my life who needed it most.

I don't know what my teacher thought of me as I stood in that line, but I suddenly felt defensive and angry that the question had even come up. *I did work.* I worked hard. I worked at home, at the grocery store, at numerous family members' homes, on the road in my minivan, and I also worked when I was at the crowded mall, in the line with my precious family, waiting to see Santa Claus!

As he and his wife prepared to go, I wished them both a very Merry Christmas. He hadn't meant to hurt my feelings, and I refused to let him know that he had.

As I suspected, the picture turned out beautifully. Those waiting in line behind us laughed when we all got in the picture. They were also full of Christmas spirit and happily took a photo of us with our camera so we could legally make copies to pass out to family and friends. Santa, though tired, remained patient.

For the rest of the afternoon, I pushed Allen around in the stroller and watched Jeff chase Anna happily through the mall. She pranced and danced in her little red dress and red shoes, and people apologized when she almost ran into them, instead of the other way around. In fact, everyone stopped their rushed shopping to ooh and aah over our beautiful babies. I felt pride and self-confidence rush through me. In that instant, with all of the people in the mall making a fuss over my babies, I faced the question about where I worked again. And this time there was no hesitation.

I raised my head high and smiled. "I am Mama to these two sweet babies—that's who I am! I work every minute of every day, and I am very, very proud of what I do!"

"Set the holiday mood each year by erecting a special Christmas decoration, such as a lighted star, that will lead the family home."

BY BILL PEARSALL

The Guiding Star

Dad was born and raised in Virginia. He met Mom in Oklahoma, when he was relocated there during World War II. Though he loved the Southwest, cowboy movies, and the wide-open spaces, he never forgot Virginia. When he passed away, we instinctively knew where he should be laid to rest. My brother, Joe, and I drove his ashes back to Virginia to be buried next to his parents.

Joe drove all night and I lay in the backseat, looking up at the stars, trying to sleep. But all I could think about was my childhood, and the star that guided my family to my grandparents' house on Christmas.

I was born shortly after the war in a small town not far from my maternal grandparents' farm. Dad worked in the oil business, as did most of my uncles, and since Mom had four sisters, family surrounded me. My grandparents' farm was named Willow Springs; my grandfather and Uncle Clyde—Mom's only brother—ran a dairy together. Every childhood memory I have is filled with pictures of that farm and my family. We gathered at the farm for Sunday dinners, Easter egg hunts, picnics, holidays, and any other reason that popped up. But the best gathering of all was Christmas Eve. In my childhood memories, the days approaching Christmas were always cold and gray—seldom snowy, just wet. And they seemed quiet . . . hushed.

A day or so before Christmas, as soon as Dad came home from work, we loaded the car with presents, food, and clothes, and drove to Willow Springs. It was about forty miles—just the right length of time for an excited young boy to be in the car. Because Willow Springs was located outside an even smaller town than the one we lived in, we had to cross the infamous Dead Man's Creek to get there. To me, the creek was a gaping canyon. There was nothing safe to me about that bridge, but as I held my breath and prayed, we always made it across. I drew a deep breath of relief and focused my attention ahead. It was smooth sailing from there on a dirt road that ran straight as an arrow right up to the farm.

As we came up over the hill, just past Dead Man's Creek, we always peered into the night, searching. Then finally, we'd spot it: a faint light far off in the distance. It was almost dark by then and the light seemed to sit in the sky like a lantern hung there just for us. As soon as my brother and I spotted the light, we'd give out a hoot and a holler, knowing our place in the universe on this sacred night.

"Like the star that guided the Three Wise Men to Jesus on the first Christmas Eve, so are we being guided," Mom explained softly, as our arms shot forward, pointing toward the light. In seconds, the light began to take shape. As always, she was right. It was a star—our very own guiding star.

Uncle Clyde had somehow affixed the star to the roof of my grandparents' house. Thinking back now, I remember how huge the star was. Though it was made out of scrap lumber—shaped into a star and covered with lights—it was a beacon to me. How Uncle Clyde ever got it onto the roof is a mystery I never tried too hard to solve. Even at that tender age, I knew if I figured it out, it would have taken away some of the magic.

We had our own star to guide us on a cold winter's night, and that's all that mattered to me.

The last part of the drive seemed to last an eternity. When we finally pulled into the driveway, I was ready to explode. The whole yard would be filled with cars, men, and children scurrying back and forth into the house carrying armloads of stuff, and women standing on the porch smiling and hugging everyone who passed within arm's reach. As a young man, I protested the hugs and kisses, but in truth I always looked forward to the attention.

Food was the order of the day at all our gatherings, but the word *Christmas* put a whole new meaning to meals. The smells of baking turkey, fresh bread, dressing, and pies of all description filled the house, along with the aroma of a hickory fire. The fireplace was my favorite spot, especially coming in from the cold.

The first evening was a flurry of activity, everyone getting ready to eat, placing presents under the tree, and preparing beds and sleeping pallets. The next day—Christmas Eve—was more of the same. Breakfast of biscuits and gravy and sausage and butter started us off for the day, and then we were bundled up and shooed out of the house to play. The farm was a whole universe to be explored, and my cousins and I took full advantage. Mostly though, we were just biding our time, waiting for the evening meal and the presents. The presents we received at our family Christmases were not large or lavish—money was not plentiful. Instead, the gifts were thoughtful handmade treasures; mementos of a slower time, a time when relationships were paramount and the world didn't get in the way.

After all was finished, my parents, aunts, uncles, and cousins loaded piles of stuff back into their cars, and soon we all headed home to wait for Santa Claus. Dad warmed up the car, and then the rest of us stepped out into the cold black night to the sound of cheerful voices shouting "Goodbye," "Merry Christmas," and "Drive carefully." The yard was lighted up like a Christmas tree, as the cars circled around and then left the driveway. Soon there would be only faint squares of light from the house windows visible beneath the bright star. Finally, just as we neared Dead Man's Creek again, the star disappeared from view.

The world seemed dark then and not only in a physical sense, but I could still see my dad's head in the front seat, silhouetted against the dashboard lights, and I felt safe knowing he was in charge. As I laid there in the backseat, covered with blankets, I rested my head on a pillow and slept contentedly. I never remember actually going into the house on Christmas Eve. But, somehow, I always woke up the next morning in my own bed and knew that Santa had come. Every Christmas morning I knew, with a certainty that filled me with confidence, that the world I lived in was filled with light and wonder.

Now, as we drive Dad home for the last time, once again I feel like a child, lying in the dark, only this time I feel very much alone. As I glance out the window and see the stars, my thoughts center on Dad. It is painful to realize that I will never again feel the safety a child feels knowing his father is at the wheel. It is painful, also, to realize that I will never again bask beneath the light of my uncle's guiding star. But at the same time, I know there is nothing to fear. The sky is full of stars, and Dad—his teachings and his guidance—will always be with me.

"For a magical treat on Christmas Day, purchase an ornament that can be opened and then hide a special gift inside of it. Make sure a different member of the family receives it each year."

BY LOY MICHAEL CERF

Speechless

Mom's eyes gleamed happily as she lifted the softball-size papier-mâché ornament out of a tissue-paper nest. "Isn't it beautiful?"

Personally, I didn't think much of it. But then as a brooding hormonal thirteen-year-old, nothing my mother did impressed me. Nonetheless, my father grinned excitedly as he reached for it.

"Um, um . . . oh, #*%$@&!" Daddy muttered in frustration.

A series of strokes had left Daddy very nearly speechless. The only word he could utter, with certainty, was a most unpleasant expletive. It shocked many strangers, but was music to familial ears; we were just glad he could communicate at all. Instantly, my teenaged heart softened.

"So you really like this decoration, Daddy?" I smiled, taking it from his hand. To my surprise, the ball opened.

"See!" Daddy chuckled. He stammered incoherently, but his rapid gesturing was crystal clear.

"I do see!" I nodded. "The ball opens, so that on Christmas you can hide a small gift inside it."

"Special gift!" he said proudly. Then pantomiming his favorite sport, baseball, he cocked his arm back, pitching it to me. "A surprise!"

As visions of sugar plums, pretty necklaces, earrings, and gift certificates to my favorite music store danced through my head, the fragile, yet promising ornament took on an entirely new perspective.

"That will be great!" I agreed, mentally rubbing my greedy hands together. "Now, I really can't wait until Christmas."

As the holiday season neared, the family was abuzz over who would get the magic ball. Quite frankly, and simply by virtue of my being the youngest child and only girl, I felt confident that the ornament would come my way that first year. But alas, I was wrong; I'd forgotten that my most precious daughter status had been lost when my eldest brother became a father. I was mightily disappointed when Mom tossed the ornament containing a cherished family heirloom to my niece. It wasn't that I had ever wanted the heirloom—there are enough antique pieces of junk in my family to placate a dozen dealers—it was more a matter of avarice.

Still, my little niece was a sweetheart, so I quickly set my sights on next year. Once more thwarted expectation hammered my heart. I couldn't be too angry though, because my romantic second brother had stuffed it with an engagement ring and proposed marriage to his girlfriend right there under the tree. To my dismay, the following year Dad sent it to my mother with a watch, which I had helped him select.

But as time passes, holiday setbacks are forgotten. Christmas traditions begin to lose their charm when one's needs and desires change—especially for a teenager. By my sixteenth Christmas, my father had suffered so many debilitating strokes that each day he drew breath was something of a miracle and his speech was down to just one curse word.

More important to this self-centered high-school student, I was the only one of my friends who couldn't drive a car. Furthermore, despite the fact that I had three, mechanically inclined and properly licensed brothers, plus a driver-in-good-standing mother, I couldn't find anyone to help me learn how to navigate a vehicle on the road. Except for my father who, amazingly enough, not only had a brand-new Chevy Nova but a valid driver's license. (Medical concerns were infinitely more relaxed in the late 1960s.)

I'll admit that the first few weeks of learning to drive beneath Dad's impaired tutelage were incredibly harrowing. I chalked up our survival to blind stupidity and an overworked guardian angel. Nevertheless, after I'd mastered basic driving skills, Dad and I had a great and glorious time traveling the city and country roads together. We'd always been close, but under the guise of *teaching Loy to drive*, Dad and I bonded even tighter. He couldn't talk, but his sense of direction was flawless. By the time Christmas rolled around again, we'd put several thousand happy miles on that car, and I was the proud owner of an Ohio driver's license.

"Now, Daddy," I lamented, "I've got to get a car of my own."

"#*%$@&" Dad sputtered in his only way of saying, "Over my dead body!"

That Nova carried marvelous memories for both of us. So, for Christmas, I found a set of hubcaps, perfect for the car. I was very proud of them and knew my father would love them as much as I did. My only regret was that they were too big for the magic ball.

That year, the holiday was especially poignant. Dad had suffered a truly death-defying heart attack and had come home from the hospital just days before Christmas. Nevertheless, as the minutes ticked away to midnight, Daddy was as excited as a little kid. So was I—I couldn't wait to give him the hubcaps. Indeed, I was so involved with presenting my gift to him, that I didn't even care who got the special ornament.

"Here, Daddy," I said, as I handed the gaily wrapped square box to him. Clumsily, and with my help, he managed to rip it open. His cheeks glowed, and he clapped his hands in appreciation. As I displayed the hubcaps for his inspection, the magic ball flopped into the empty box beside me.

"What's this?" I exclaimed, sure someone had accidentally dropped it my way.

Daddy grinned, motioning me to open it, which I did at lightning speed. Inside was a blue key.

I looked up at Daddy. "I don't understand." The whole family was silent as I searched each face for an answer. Mom's eyes were glistening. Daddy winked and hitched his thumb over his shoulder toward the front door. Curious, I sprang up and opened the door. To my total shock, the Nova, which was parked in the driveway, had a huge red bow fastened to its roof! It took a minute for the news to sink in. But when it did, I whooped for joy.

Looking at Daddy, I asked, "That key . . . it's to the Nova, and the car . . . you're giving it to me?"

Grinding his teeth against his tears, Daddy simply nodded his head. Overjoyed, I hugged his frail shoulders as hard as I dared. Through my own tears, I whispered, "Thank you, Daddy, and Merry Christmas."

Daddy touched his heart and then pointed to me. "#*%$@&," he replied.

I smiled and repeated the sentiments I knew he meant but couldn't say. "I love you, too, Daddy," I said as I kissed him. Then we both grabbed our coats and within minutes were seated in the Nova—*my* Nova. Dad grinned, his eyes shiny with excitement as he watched me hang the magic Christmas ball from the review mirror. Turning, he waved goodbye to our family, nodding proudly as I carefully backed out of the driveway.

> *"It's never to late to make a*
> *difference in someone else's life."*

BY CAROL NYMAN

A Change of Attitude

C hristmas was fast approaching, and I was self-absorbed, adjusting to my husband's passing three months earlier. I particularly missed the board games we pulled from the closet each year, and at the moment the thought of hibernating until after New Year's was very appealing.

A week before Christmas, I took a long look at my pitiful self and decided I needed an attitude adjustment. Reluctantly, I shoved my pity pot aside and began to dig out the decorations. I moved the furniture, made room for the huge seven-foot artificial tree in the corner where we always put it, and started decorating. As I pulled each treasure from the tissue, I listened to the Christmas music coming from the radio and let the tears flow freely. There were so many memories wrapped in those tissue treasures.

It was late in the evening when I stepped back to admire my handiwork. Reveling in the beauty of the transformed living room, my heart warmed. I slept that night for the first time in months.

On Christmas Eve, I went shopping for ingredients to make a small holiday dinner for myself. In a passing conversation with one of the clerks, she mentioned the store would be open on Christmas and she would miss seeing her children's delight when they found the gifts Santa had left. She was philosophical about working but glad her parents would be able to share the moment with her children.

On the way home, I began to wonder how many people had to work on Christmas and how they celebrated the holidays. I decided to find out. I stopped at the ATM and withdrew five $20 bills and tucked them into my pocket. At home, I watched the end of the eleven o'clock news and thought about the money I had withdrawn. I was excited but didn't really have a plan. An hour later I found myself on the road.

My first stop was at one of those quick-stop markets. I went inside, picked up a bag of potato chips and some dip, and went to the counter where an older woman stood. We started talking. She didn't mind working, she said, she had no family close by and no money to fly cross-country. She was charming and witty, and the conversation was delightful. Before I left, I reached into my pocket and pulled a bill out.

"Thank you for sharing this evening," I said. "This is the first holiday since my husband died and I have found it difficult. You've brightened my life—please accept this holiday 'tip.' Perhaps it will help to pay the extra charges on your phone bill when you call your family. Happy holidays!"

Tears flooded my eyes as I backed out of the lot and headed to another location. I found two other businesses open, and with each I shared my holiday tip.

The next morning when I awoke before dawn, I realized I still had $40 in my pocket. I grabbed two Christmas cards and tucked $20 in each of them, adding a personal note. This time I found a bakery using their ovens to cook turkeys and hams for their customers and a fish market open for those who wanted fresh seafood brought from the docks that morning. I listened as shop owners and employees shared stories of the holiday season, how they found time for family members and still served the community. Their enthusiasm for the holiday knew no bounds. Their eyes watered when they were given an envelope with a holiday tip inside.

The warmth I felt that Christmas was like nothing I had ever experienced. Sharing special moments with people who make our lives easier during the holidays was magical for me. It wasn't the size of the tip I offered that mattered, it was the moment of human bonding in an often forgetful world. That Christmas changed my attitude for the rest of my life. Best of all, I made a lasting friendship with the first woman I met that year on my holiday mission.

One year, wanting to give as well as receive, my new friend accompanied me on my holiday "tip" excursion. Together, we joyfully shared the same Christmas warmth we'd experienced years before, all over again.

"As the snow falls gently outside the window this holiday season, bring the magic indoors by teaching a child the fine art of cutting out paper snowflakes."

BY MICHELLE CIARLO-HAYES

White Paper Snowflakes

At the age of six, my grandfather, James, stood in the open doorway and peered out at what remained of the family Christmas tree. No one noticed. As the youngest of eleven children, James was used to going partially, if not entirely, unnoticed.

James swallowed hard as his gaze wandered over the shattered glass ornaments embedded in the bent and broken branches. The handmade snowflakes he and his brothers and sisters had cut from paper and strung together with twine grew damp and unsalvageable as they fluttered helplessly against the dirty snow. James had been particularly proud of his snowflake, even if he had needed a bit of help from his oldest sister who had held his small hands in hers and guided the sharp blades over the paper. James blinked to stop himself from remembering. It was of no matter now. The tree was out in the snow, ejected by his father in yet another of his drunken rages.

At that moment, James, who would one day be my grandfather, decided that when he had children he'd make sure Christmas would always be something spectacular.

He never went back on that vow.

There was never a man more committed to the cause of Father Christmas than Grandfather. After the birth of his first child, he decided Santa Claus would not only bring gifts on Christmas Eve, he would also bring the tree, the trains underneath, and every possible adornment for the home, inside and out! It was a stupendous undertaking, but it worked. While other families began decorating for Christmas shortly after Thanksgiving, my grandfather insisted he had a very special relationship with Mr. Claus, and that Santa would personally decorate their home when he slid down that chimney on December 24th.

Mom laughs as she recalls how her father managed the task. With the help of gallons of coffee, Grandfather—complete in Santa suit and beard, in case one of the children awoke—took on a month's worth of preparations in a single night! He ran out and purchased the tree, strung the lights inside and out, hung the ornaments, put batteries in presents that required them, and finally, assembled the trains. Given the fact that his to-do list as well as the assembly of the train set—a mammoth system of rails and engines—did not begin until two or three in the morning, it usually meant that several of my great-uncles would be roused from their beds by frantic phone calls from a half-asleep Santa, begging for their assistance.

They always came, no matter the time. And Christmas morning was always perfect, complete with white paper snowflakes hanging from the branches of the tree. No one ever noticed the dark circles under my grandfather's eyes, or the fact that he had to stifle several yawns during Mass. Everyone was too overjoyed. The glittering tree, roaring trains, and bulging stockings—now hung over a crackling fire—greeted them as they stood at the bottom of their stairs, their hair still uncombed, their eyes glowing with excitement.

My mother did not insist Santa Claus bring our tree with him on his Christmas Eve delivery, nor did she insist he erect a complex rail system in a single evening. But every year, she sat with me and guided my hands as I cut shapes from folded white paper. When I grew old enough, she sat back and told me the stories of her father's crazy Christmas antics. As I made snowflakes for our tree, I always thought of Grandfather standing there that night, as he watched his dreams of a perfect Christmas morning dissolve in the snow like his paper snowflake. But, rather than being consumed by sadness, my grandfather kept his promise to give his children the loving holiday they deserved, and for that, I will always be grateful.

"Getting together as a family during the holidays is as special a treat as receiving the finest Christmas gift."

BY PATRICIA HOPPER

Christmas in the Rare Aul' Times

Leaving Dublin, Ireland, to live in the United States meant missing out on Christmas with my parents and five siblings. To complicate matters, three more siblings left home to live on the golden shores of Australia. After that, it became rare that our family was ever complete. What held us close were those threaded years of growing up together. As distance drove us apart, we depended on phone calls and letters to keep us connected. Around Christmastime, conversations with my parents became more nostalgic than usual.

"Ahh, Patricia," my dad would say. "Your mam and I were just saying how nice it would be if we had you all here for Christmas, the way it used to be. Do you remember the time when..."

I did remember. One particular Christmas, when I was eleven, my father asked me to meet him at his office to help him carry home the presents for my younger siblings. It was cold and windy, as we braved our way to a small toy-store in Meath Street.

"I have everything ready for you, Shea," a burly man said when we went inside. He pulled two parcels out from behind the counter, one larger than the other. Boxes of various sizes were stacked, wrapped in brown paper, and tied together with string.

"This must be your eldest girl." The man held out a thick hand. "Think you can manage this parcel, young lady?"

"Yes," I said, gripping a parcel that was heavier than it looked.

He noticed and looped some twine several times on top of the parcel to make a handle. He motioned me to pick up it again. "See if that's better," he said. I did and smiled.

"We'd best be going," Dad said. "The Missus is waiting for us to get home."

The shopkeeper grinned. "Know what you mean, Shea. Thanks for the business, and a happy and Holy Christmas to you and yours."

My dad turned to me. "Well, Patricia, it's up to us now to get these presents home." We walked back down Meath Street and on to Thomas Street to catch the bus.

On the corner, a woman sat in a doorway, wrapped in a dirty black shawl, her lined face, expressionless, beneath its folds. On a piece of cloth were some coins that passersby had thrown down. This was not an unusual sight in the city. Others, like this woman, sat on busy streets and bridges. When I asked why people did this, Dad explained vaguely that they had special problems.

My dad had spent everything he had on the presents we now struggled with, except for our bus fare home. He looked at the woman and then at the coins he held ready. It was Christmas, and he wanted to be generous. Knowing I wouldn't be able to lug my parcel the five miles home, he asked, "Can you walk from the church?" This was still over a mile from our house, and the parcel was heavy, but I didn't want to appear selfish.

"I can make it," I said.

"Good." He counted out what we needed for bus fare and dropped the rest in front of the woman.

"Merry Christmas," Dad said.

"God bless you," the woman muttered.

I was glad to find a seat on the bus. I stared out the window as we left the city slowly behind. It was dark now, and I wondered if we would make it home before the sleeting rain that had been threatening all day began. At our bus stop, the conductor wished us Merry Christmas and helped us off the platform with our parcels. All we had left was the trek home.

When we reached our front door, Dad pushed open the letterbox lid, and put his ear against it. Voices came from inside. "They're not in the kitchen," he whispered. He flipped the lid twice. It was a signal to my mother, who had been getting anxious that we hadn't come home yet.

I heard her say, "Margaret, Collette, Jimmy, come and get your cake." We listened to feet thundering toward the kitchen, and when we heard one voice tell another "His piece is bigger than mine," Dad put his key in the lock.

We tiptoed upstairs, stored the parcels safely in the wardrobe, and slipped back outside. We began talking loudly when we opened the front door a second time.

On Christmas Eve, we went to Mass. In the quiet dimly lighted church, while reverently listening to the haunting hymns, I thought of the woman sitting on the cold pavement and wondered if she had a warm home, someone to care for her, a family. Seeing the bright, excited faces of my brothers and sisters kneeling beside me, I put disagreements aside and was grateful for them.

My younger siblings went to bed in anticipation of Santa Claus. Later, when they were asleep, we brought the toys from their hiding place and placed them gently beneath the Christmas tree. Afterward, my parents, my older brother, Stephen, and I dressed for bed. As soon as we were in our beds, my dad did what he had always done; he woke my little brother and sisters and told them Santa had just left with his reindeer!

Dad rushed downstairs leading Margaret, Collette, and Jimmy in exclamations of delight at the toys under the Christmas tree, as if seeing them for the first time. My mother, always the practical one, complained, "I wish he'd wait till morning like normal people. He knows you'll be too excited to sleep, and you'll be exhausted tomorrow."

Those memories sifted through my mind last Christmas Eve, as I thought about my upcoming visit to Ireland, scheduled for right after Christmas. I was going home to be with my parents and my youngest brother, Noel, who was visiting with his family from Australia. That night, around 2 A.M., the phone rang. It was my sister Margaret calling. I thought she had confused the time difference.

"I'll be home—" I began.

She cut me short. "Dad's gone."

For a moment, my heart stopped. "I'll be there as soon as I can," I said.

We were all together within thirty-six hours. On December 28, we walked into our parish church, where my father's coffin had been interred, to say our last goodbyes. My father's favorite song echoed the past, "Ring a ring a rosy . . . remember Dublin City in the rare aul' times." Taking our places in the front pew, I felt my father's presence and could sense his pride that the whole family was there. His lighthearted voice echoed in my heart. "Ahh, Patricia, your mam and I are delighted to have you all here for the Christmas, the way it used to be. Do you remember the time when...."

"Find time to be with the one you love, even if it's only to visit a sick relative, or to watch a television program. Do it together, and do it for no other reason than because you love one another."

BY EVAN GUILFORD-BLAKE

First Christmas

In 2000, I spent my first Christmas as a married man.

That, I'm sure, doesn't seem a terribly unusual event, but I was fifty-three—well beyond the age when most men marry for the first time. And I spent that holiday, in an unusual manner.

My wife, Roxanna, and I used our holiday vacation to visit her seventy-nine-year-old father, a patient in a long-term care facility about half an hour from Daytona. He suffered from an Alzheimer's-like condition, which had left him unable to stand or speak, and while he seemed to recognize familiar faces, he was no longer able to identify them. Sometimes, his eyes would follow movement. Sometimes, they seemed glued to the television set, which always seemed to be on. Sometimes, he'd smile when my wife—or anyone else—spoke to him or fed him; but, for all practical purposes, Roxanna—his thirty-seven-year-old daughter—had become a virtual stranger.

Visiting him was difficult for her, and the difficulty was always compounded by the eight-hour drive from Atlanta. We checked into our motel the evening of December 23, made a brief visit to the nursing home—where we discovered he had just been put on a diet of puréed food, due to newly worsened respiratory problems—ate a quiet dinner, and collapsed exhausted into bed. Christmas Eve was more of the same. We visited for several hours, talked with the staff and other patients, dispensed among them the box of chocolates we'd brought for my father-in-law (his favorite food, but something his new regimen prohibited), and tried to remain upbeat. But the stress, combined with the fact that we'd moved two days before the trip and our new apartment had been in complete chaos when we'd climbed into the car, had left us both frayed. We decided to spend Christmas Eve—our first Christmas Eve together—quietly in our motel room, which we'd decorated with a six-inch crepe-paper Christmas tree.

This might seem a sad celebration to some, but for us it became an affirmation. Feeling overwhelmed by all we'd just gone through, frazzled, and even a little depressed by our impending Christmas Day visit to the nursing home, we turned on the television. This was an unusual event since I hadn't owned one in thirty years, and Roxanna spent less than an hour a month before her thirteen-inch black-and-white. Fortunately, we had the luck to discover the rebroadcast of an old *Perry Como Christmas Special*, a particularly nostalgic ninety minutes for me, because it recalled the living room of my childhood, where years ago my parents and I had sat watching Como singing. He was my mother's favorite singer and my wife's mother's as well. We both cried, lying on the king-size bed, our heads leaning on each other's shoulders. Sentimentality? Without doubt. But, for the first time in the season, we both felt nudged by the Christmas spirit. Now and then, we sang along, softly and badly, but with the peculiar pleasure of the "we" the moment asserted.

When the special ended, we remembered we hadn't eaten. There were no open restaurants nearby—not even the fast-food places were serving barely an hour before Christmas—so we walked a few blocks to a gas station and bought a dinner of crackers, tortilla chips, cheese dip, salsa, and a couple bottles of beer. We went back to our room and sat before our tree, a single pillar candle for light. We ate and talked and held hands. And we marveled at our good fortune to have found each other in the odd manner we did—online, at a site where, had I logged on five minutes earlier or later, we'd probably never have met—at a moment in both of our lives when developing *the* relationship seemed improbable. At midnight, we opened a few gifts, admired them and each other, blew out the candle, went to bed, and held each other close.

Now, each year, no matter where we are or what other accoutrements of the season we may have, we set our tiny tree before our fireplace, light a candle, put on a Perry Como record, sit, talk, and remember.

My married friends say they're used to shared Christmases and, as the years have passed, Christmases have become pleasantly routine for me, too. Yes, I've had more exciting ones that I've spent thoroughly engulfed by the paraphernalia and the tidings of comfort and joy. But that Christmas, perhaps the simplest, coming at a time when I was as exhausted as I'd ever been, will always be the most memorable.

Marriage is a simple gift, sometimes exhausting gift, that is taken for granted all too often. I know I'd *thought* that before, but that Christmas Eve is when it became clear to me, shining beautifully, like that star in the East, through the clear and loving eyes of my new wife.

"A wonderful way to show children how many days until Christmas finally arrives is to include the Advent Calendar in your holiday activities."

BY SUZANNE WARING

The Advent Calendar

"It's my turn. Give it to me!"

"It's mine! You hung the angel yesterday. I'm going to do it."

"No, you put up both Mr. and Mrs. Snowman. I'm putting up Santa. Give it to me or I'll tell!"

It was Christmas Eve, and the argument between our two young sons had been going on all day, turning our home into a distinct contrast to the idyllic picture of a family on the night before Christmas. Instead of two perfectly behaved little boys—already dressed for bed—sitting on their dad's lap while he read the Christmas story, dissension over who would hang Santa on the Advent Calendar had ensued, destroying the perfect vision that danced in my head.

My mother-in-law had spent a year making the calendar, so that she could send it to her grandsons in time for Advent. The calendar was a wall hanging of a perfectly symmetrical Christmas tree on a white-felt background. Twenty-four gold knobs were attached to the tree in places where ornaments were to be hung.

Beginning on the first day of December, and every day after that, the boys took one Christmas ornament and chose which gold knob to hang it on. The number of ornaments left to be hung on the tree told the boys how many days were left until the holiday. When only one ornament remained, they knew Christmas would be the next day.

With hangers of thin gold string, the three-dimensional ornaments were tiny and extremely colorful. In addition to the angel, Santa, and Mr. and Mrs. Snowman, the ornaments included a chorister, a soldier, a teddy bear, a clown, and a rabbit. There were also bells, candy canes, bulbs, candles, birds, and a chapel. The Advent Calendar held a prominent place in our family room and became more noticeable each day as the beautiful ornaments added color and depth.

I could imagine the many hours my mother-in-law spent cutting and sewing the little ornaments. Each had been created out of tiny pieces of felt, gold braid, and sequins. The project must have taken hours under a strong light with needle and thread.

Unbeknownst to me, the boys had decided to leave the angel and Santa to be hung last. Two days prior to Christmas, the angel was hung at the very top of the Christmas tree. Now only Santa remained to be hung in the middle of the tree just below the angel, and both boys wanted to do the honors.

My husband looked at our nine-year-old, "What year were you born?" he asked quietly.

"1970," Kelly replied.

"And you were born in 1973, right?" he said to Keith who nodded in agreement.

"Well, now," Leonard said, "one of you was born during an even year and one was born during an odd year. Who was born in the even year?"

Kelly yelped, "Me!"

Leonard smiled and looked at Keith. "And who was born in an odd year?"

"Me!" said Keith, pointing to his chest and copying his older brother.

Then my husband took out a piece of paper and wrote on it: *Kelly Bryan will hang Santa on the even years, and Keith Edward will hang Santa on the odd years.* He placed the note in the box of ornaments.

Kelly looked at his little brother. "All right, Keith, this is an odd year, so you hang the Santa. I hung the angel last night."

In the years that followed, the boys looked forward to getting out the Advent Calendar. They developed a pattern for the sequence in which the ornaments were hung and where to place each ornament. My mother-in-law took pleasure in knowing how involved they were with decorating the tree with the small ornaments.

When the boys went off to college, they took out the Advent Calendar on Thanksgiving, when they were home for the holiday, and then I hung the ornaments each day until they came home again for Christmas vacation. Some days, I forgot or hurriedly hung several at a time—something that would have never happened before the boys went away to school! Since I had never figured out the boys' sequence for putting each ornament on the tree, it was never the same twice during the years I was in charge.

As soon as the boys returned home from college—or from wherever their careers had taken them—the ornaments mysteriously returned to their "correct" places, and more often then not, one would comment on whether it was an even or odd year.

In December 2000, my mother-in-law, Dorothy, passed away during Advent. It was difficult for the family to finish decorating the calendar that year. As each ornament was hung, we thought about how much the labors of her handiwork represented the love she had for her grandchildren. We hung the ornaments that year and in the years since to honor her.

Time changes traditions, and one *even* year came that our older son chose to stay in his new home many states away over the Christmas holiday. It was a natural and good transition for him and his wife. It also meant that he wouldn't be at our house to celebrate the holiday and to hang Santa the night before Christmas. When I opened the box of tiny ornaments and found the note my husband had written so many years ago, tears stung my eyes. Our little boys had grown up and had lives of their own now. Our day-to-day time with them had come and gone.

As I recovered from that sudden wave of nostalgia, I reminded myself that an old tradition perhaps leads to an ever better new tradition. Someday, we would have little children in our family again. And when that day comes, I know they will want to decorate the Advent Calendar with the tiny ornaments made so very long time ago by their great-grandmother. When that day comes, my grandchildren will find their own way of putting the ornaments on the calendar just as Dorothy's grandchildren had.

"As you add strands and strands of colored lights to your Christmas tree this year, include one blinking blue light to represent the star in the East."

BY SHIRLEY P. GUMERT

The Light in the East

I t was a rare exciting Christmas Eve. Our son and daughter had called to say that their families—both living many miles away—would be coming home for the holidays! My husband, John, and I raced to the store in search of a tall spruce tree. Excitement flowed through us when we found exactly what we were looking for. We filled grocery carts, did some hasty house-cleaning, wrapped a few gifts, and set out boxes and boxes of stored tree ornaments.

As we sat impatiently in front of the fireplace, listening for the sound of car tires crunching on our gravel driveway, I remembered other Christmases, when John and I had been a much younger couple. Then we were the ones traveling with our children to the town where four grandparents waited. I opened an old box of ornaments and set aside a few fragile glass ones to put into a crystal bowl. Then, as I lifted out a string of tangled Christmas lights, my mind went back in time to a memory so vivid it was as if it were taking place right before my eyes.

I remembered Tom Andrew, John's father. Every holiday season he handled the lights. As he struggled to untangle each string and twisted every bulb, his exclamations turned the air blue! In those years, if one bulb was loose or burned out, the whole string stayed dark.

"Maybe it's the wiring," John would say, as he came across a string that didn't work. Hoping his suggestion would sink in, he would add, "Maybe we should buy new strings."

"No!" His dad was always adamant. "These worked last year; they'll be fine."

Knowing there was nothing he could do to make his father see reason, John would shake his head. "I'll go down to the dime store and try to find a few new bulbs like these," John would mutter. He wanted out.

Meanwhile, our kids sat hunched on the floor, underneath the unadorned Christmas tree, watching their grandfather conduct his annual battle. Throughout the evening, Tom continued his strategy of detangling strings, twisting and turning bulbs, searching for extension cords, and reaching for a glass of the same jug wine he'd used to soak the fruitcakes he'd made several weeks earlier. (Tom Andrew made great fruitcakes.)

Until the light strings all worked, the Christmas celebration could not begin. The tree decorating had to wait. The presents were not allowed under the tree, and the bountiful trays of snack foods could not be set out. Everything remained at a standstill. Thankfully, the moment always came, and when it did, Tom Andrew's smile was as bright as the light display. His efforts were met with sighs and shouts by everyone in the house!

One year our young son pointed up at the decorated tree. "That light," he said with trepidation. "That one blue light is blinking." He looked at me worriedly. "Is it burning out? Will we have to find another bulb? Will all our lights go out?"

I hugged him reassuringly and hoped the light held its own.

It did. That funny blue light—different from all the rest—just continued to blink. We decided it was special, like the star in the East. The next year, the same light blinked, and again the next year, and again the next, until our growing kids couldn't wait to see that one special light each Christmas. When it finally burned out, Tom Andrew found a small box, labeled it, and packed the light away. He never threw anything out and never bought fancy new strings of lights either. I suppose he was thinking someday he'd get that blinking blue light to work again.

When our parents' homes became the places of Christmases Past, all of Tom Andrew's lights came in a carton to our house along with the memories of a lifetime. I remember on late nights, when Christmas tree bulbs shone brightly, how Tom Andrew, seated in his deep red leather chair, would prop his feet onto his footstool, and turn on his reading lamp. After he selected from his stack of books, with grandchildren curled beside him, he'd read aloud from Robert Louis Stevenson's *Treasure Island* (the one with N. C. Wyeth's illustrations), or J. Frank Dobie's *Coronado's Children*, Rudyard Kipling, or the poems of Robert Service, which were also favorites. Grandchildren would listen to the comforting sound of his voice and watch the blue Christmas light, blink, blink, blinking, until they too blinked out for the night.

This year, many years later, as our children joined us for Christmas, John and I happily got out our accumulation of Christmas tree decorations. We all smiled at the surprise our son brought—fancy new strands of lights. While our daughter set out trays of vegetables and dip, our three grandchildren helped string the many lights and hang the tinsel and ornaments. We set out piles of gifts and bountiful trays of food—even a fruitcake. Happily, there wasn't any problem lighting the tree.

Later that night, however, our son, who now held the battered copy of *Coronado's Children*, pointed toward the tree. One blue light had begun blinking. It was not the light of old, but to us it was a special signal. It was as if our past Christmases had returned to shine on as a beacon of family tradition and timelessness. As if Tom Andrew and all of the Christmas antics our family had ever found important surrounded us at that moment, reminding us once again that Christmas Present is a beautiful continuation of Christmas Past.

"Starting a tradition doesn't have to be anything big. It doesn't have to cost a lot of money or stress everyone out. A Christmas tradition can be as simple as giving everyone a hug as they enter your home on Christmas Day, or it can be as complicated as putting on an entire theater production."

BY CATHERINE LANSER

Playing with Tradition

I've probably been asked a million times, but for some reason whenever someone asks me about Christmas, I always get a little stuck. The conversation usually happens sometime in November, after the Halloween decorations are packed away and before the light radio stations start playing Christmas carols. The question is simple, something as innocuous as, "What does your family do for Christmas? Do you have any special traditions?"

I know how to answer the first part of the question, but the second part always leaves me stumped. My family has been doing the same thing on Christmas Eve for as long as I can remember, but the word *tradition* seems too formal for my family. We're a big loud group of regular people, who get together, eat appetizers, and open presents. We couldn't possibly know anything about something as esoteric as *tradition,* could we? To me traditions look something like a photo shoot from *Better Homes and Gardens*, which is definitely not the Christmas I know.

From two turtledoves engaged on Christmas—more than fifty years ago—to an original family of nine children, to a menagerie nearly as big as the total gifts given in "The Twelve Days of Christmas," our family isn't about formality. So when asked about our family traditions, I mumble something about not really having any. But once, when I barely mentioned something about singing and a play to a new friend, I was pressed for more details.

"Wait, there's a play?" she asked.

There it was. *Tradition.* Staring me right in the face.

We're not exactly the Osmonds, so you wouldn't expect music and performance to take center stage at our Christmas celebration, but somehow it has. I guess that's one thing about traditions. Like Christmas decorations, traditions are intimately related to the occasion they celebrate. Something that seems so normal at one time of the year can seem so out of place at another.

Music and performance became part of our Christmas tradition when my oldest nephews, now in their twenties, were still boys. My sister-in-law Leslie would line them up to sing "Must Be Santa" with Mitch Miller and the Gang. As more cousins were born, the performance grew, until it was something we always did. It opened up our once-reserved family and gave rise to the production that now is Christmas Eve.

As Leslie cues the music, the children take their places at the front of the room. In earlier years, anxious parents stood in the back of the room helping their children with the words and accompanying motions, but that's no longer necessary. Now, the adults are free to join in the fun. And we all do, bobbing around and laughing "ho-ho-ho," until we're not faking at all. By the time the song is done, we're thoroughly warmed up for what has become the focal point of the evening.

I'm not sure what year the children's Christmas play started, but it has become an irreplaceable component of our celebration. It began simply as a dramatic re-enactment of the birth of Baby Jesus. As the children have come into their own personalities, however, it has taken a more dramatic turn. Once created on the fly right before the presentation, the play now involves weeks of preparation by my preteen nieces, which includes a slew of e-mails and phone calls to coordinate the big event.

Over the years, the play has veered from the straight re-enactment of Scripture to a more avant-garde modern-day morality retelling that even includes live musical accompaniment. The props, once as simple as blankets to denote a shepherd's garb, have become more sophisticated and worldly—such as a feather boa to portray the girl who has everything. In addition to presents, my sisters and brothers now chuckle as they carry in garbage bags full of props, keyboards, drum sets, and even miniature Christmas trees, when they arrive for the evening.

The play takes place in the cramped space between the couch and the fireplace in my brother's living room. The adults and older cousins gather round, as if watching some sort of street performance. A hush falls over the crowd and the play begins. After a short while, it usually begins again, because when you've been preparing for something as long as you have been for this, you want it to go smoothly. If someone has just been given their lines a few minutes ago, they may make a mistake. Maybe someone forgot that the younger kids can't read their lines, because they can't read yet. Nonetheless after a few false starts, the performers always hit their stride. Although it's not ready for Broadway, it never disappoints this audience.

During the production, I see how we, like the play, have grown and transformed. Brothers and sisters are now mothers and fathers, and babies are growing into sophisticated young adults. Through it all, this tradition is our mainstay.

After the show, the Christmas celebration proceeds. Presents are opened, food is eaten, more laughs are shared and, at the end of the night, we're all satisfied, tired, and ready to go to bed. We're also a little sad that it's over, and every one of us is looking forward to doing it all again the next year.

I guess that's it. That's what tradition is all about. It's the thing you look forward to, the thing that will put the biggest smile on your face when you gather around various kitchen tables years from now. It isn't necessarily stuffy or pristine. And sometimes it even has a little dramatic flair.

Like homemade ornaments, holiday traditions can be sweet, cute, unique, or even a little odd. But because these special times—whether created by a whole family or just one person—are filled with love and continue to be shared from year to year, Christmas traditions are the most precious gifts we can give ourselves.

Contributors

Nancy Allan ("The Thank-You Kiss") won a manicure set in third grade for a story she wrote about her class. She never stopped writing. For twenty-eight years, Nancy was a reporter and news editor for the *Greenfield Observer* newspaper. When she retired, the city threw her a retirement party. Nancy still writes a column for her condo newspaper, and her poetry has appeared many times in *Wisconsin Poet's Calendar*.

Kathryn Arnold ("Table Gifts") was raised in Washington and has lived in California and Costa Rica. Kathryn was a newspaper reporter and editor at the *Westlock Co.* newspaper and also reported for the *Latin American Tribune* in Costa Rica. Currently, she has two novels in progress.

Trish Ayers ("Finding the Perfect Tree") has had three short stories published in *The Rocking Chair Reader Anthology Series*. In addition, she has had poetry published in journals, books, and in several theatrical pieces—one of which was performed in New York City. Her plays—recognized four years running by the Appalachian Writers' Association— have toured the United States as well as Japan.

Nadja Meri Bernitt ("The Red Velvet Stocking") holds a master's degree in writing from the State University of New York, at Stony Brook, where she also taught writing. Her work appears in a variety of anthologies, as well as in *Dana Literary Online Journal*, the *Tampa Tribune,* and the *Sarasota Herald Tribune*.

Amber Brecht ("Angels We Have Heard on High") has had her work appear on television, radio, and the Internet, as well as in newspapers and magazines across the county. She worked in television news and films before joining the West Gallery in Taos, New Mexico, as vice president/director. Amber is currently a freelance writer and grant consultant in Southern California.

Cynthia Brian ("Gifts of the Magi") is the bestselling coauthor of *Chicken Soup for the Gardener's Soul*, the author of four books, and is an internationally acclaimed keynote speaker, lifestyle expert, TV / radio personality, and syndicated columnist. With three decades of experience in the entertainment field, she has performed with some of the biggest names in the industry. Find more information at *www.cynthiabrian.com* or *www.bethestaryouare.org*.

Diane Buller ("Staying Home with Scarlatina") has always lived in central Illinois. For more than thirty years, she taught high school and college writing. Finally, she is practicing what she's preached in the classroom. Diane and her husband, Gary, have two college-age children. She still loves to sing Christmas carols.

Rebecca Burgener ("Pictures with Santa") lives in Knoxville, Tennessee, with her husband and two children. She divides her time between her family (immediate and extended), a part-time job, and the literature magazine she has started. For more information or to contact Rebecca Burgener, visit *www.pondripplesmag.com*.

Dorothy L. Bussemer ("Oyster Stew with Mother") was born in Zanesville, Ohio. She holds a degree in social science and economics. Among other interests, she enjoys world travel, cooking, and, of course, writing—especially Christmas stories. Dorothy believes that with faith in God and country the best is yet to be.

Loy Michael Cerf ("Speechless") is an avid writer. Her most recent sales include *A Cup of Comfort for Dog Lovers* ("The Anti Alpha Male") and *A Cup of Comfort for Cat Lovers* ("Ozzie to the Rescue"). When she isn't traveling with her husband, Loy crochets blankets for Project Linus.

Ruth Coe Chambers ("Of Books and Dogs and Dreams Coming True"), the author of *The Chinaberry Album*, has published short stories and articles in various magazines and written two award-winning plays.

A psychology graduate from California State University, Fresno, Ruth is listed in Marquis *Who's Who of American Women* and *Who's Who in America*. For more information, visit her at *www.ruthcchambers.com*.

Michelle Ciarlo-Hayes ("White Paper Snowflakes") is a freelance writer living in Elkins Park, Pennsylvania. She finds time to write when her husband, Marty, is at home to wrangle their two wonderful, yet very active, boys, Danny and Lucas.

Sally Clark ("Christmas Shells") celebrates Christmas at her home in Fredericksburg, Texas, with her husband, children, and grandchildren. Her stories have appeared in *A Cup of Comfort for Weddings* and *A Cup of Comfort for Horse Lovers*. She has also written children's stories, poetry, greeting cards, and humor for various publications.

Joan Clayton ("Love Notes on My Tree") is a retired elementary teacher, and her husband, Emmitt, is a retired high school principal. They were high school sweethearts, and will soon be celebrating their sixtieth wedding anniversary. Joan is the religion columnist for her local newspaper and has authored eight books. More information about her writing can be found at *www.joanclayton.com*.

Patricia F. D'Ascoli ("The Best Christmas Ever") is a freelance writer who publishes *Connecticut Muse*, a literary newsletter that celebrates contemporary Connecticut authors. Patricia is the author of *Diary of a Mediocre Mom: Why I Hate Water Parks and Other Mid-Life Musings*. She lives in Connecticut with her husband and three sons.

Carlene Rae Dater ("The Funnies") started her writing career twenty-five years ago and has published six books and more than 250 pieces of short fiction and nonfiction. Carlene and Dennis, her husband of thirty-eight years, are retired and live in the outskirts of San Diego, California, with their dog, Tara, the world's largest Labrador retriever.

Charlene A. Derby ("Bayberry Memories") is a freelance writer living in Southern California with her husband and son. She and her sisters still enjoy serving each other breakfast, when they get together. Her previously published stories have appeared in several compilation books and in the magazines *Reminisce Extra* and *Focus on the Family*.

Barbara Farland ("Trash to Treasure") became a freelance writer in 2007, after more than fifteen years in business communications. It's been smooth sailing so far, thanks to her quiet New Hope, Minnesota, home and daily breaks spent knitting. Barbara's prized knitting-needle collection resides in the now famous wood box restored by her husband, Terry. Visit Barbara's website at *www.barbarafarland.com*.

Lisa Finch ("A New Tradition") holds an Honors English BA from McMaster University. She has been published locally and also in the recently released anthology *Living the Serenity Prayer* (Adams Media). She lives in Forest, Ontario, with her wonderful and supportive husband, Chris, and their three beautiful children, Hailey, Matthew, and Ben.

Pat Gallant ("Piano Solo") is a fourth-generation native New Yorker and mother to one son. Her work has appeared in publications such as the *Saturday Evening Post, Writer's Digest, New Press Literary Quarterly,* and numerous anthologies. Pat recently completed a book of literary nonfiction shorts called *Holding on to Right-Side Up.*

Pam Giordano ("Nona, Nuts, and Nostalgia") is a retired schoolteacher who resides in Bethlehem, Pennsylvania. She is a published author, whose passion is writing about her early days growing up in the ethnic neighborhoods of the south side of Bethlehem. Pam's interests include gardening, painting, and being a grandmother to twenty-one grandchildren.

Rosemary Goodwin ("Holly Berry Dreams") was born in the lovely country town of Bury St. Edmunds, in Suffolk County, England. You can see her hometown on her website *www.Rosemary-Goodwin.com.* After moving to the United States with her military husband, Rosemary lived in New England. Currently, she lives in a historic town in eastern Pennsylvania.

Elaine K. Green ("Observations from the Edge: Christmas on the Lower Nine") is a freelance writer, avid reader, and native New Orleanian. She and her husband, Eddie, have one daughter, Kelli.

Evan Guilford-Blake ("First Christmas") is an award-winning playwright, poet, and short story writer (for adults and children). His plays have been produced internationally; two are published by Playscripts, two more are forthcoming from small presses. Evan and Roxanna, a freelance writer and jewelry designer, live with their lovable, dumb-as-dirt doves Quill and Gabriella.

Shirley P. Gumert ("The Light in the East") is a freelance writer, who lives in west Kerr County, Texas. As a writer for the *Santa Fe Reporter*, Shirley won first-place awards from New Mexico Press Women and New Mexico Press Association. She has also written for the *Houston Chronicle*, and has stories in the *Rocking Chair Reader, Coming Home*, and in *Classic Christmas: True Stories of Holiday*.

Dixon Hearne ("The Rudolph Sweater") teaches and writes in Southern California. His work includes stories in recent issues of Mature Living, *the Louisiana* Review, *Kennesaw Review,* and in *Louisiana Literature, Humor for the Boomer's Heart, Roanoke Review,* and *Rockford Review.* Dixon has received several awards for short fiction. His new short story collection, *Tethered Hearts*, is forthcoming from a university press.

M. DeLoris Henscheid ("Macaroni Necklaces and Cumbersome Pride") is the sixth of eight consecutive generations of women in her family who have lived in Blackfoot, Idaho. She is the mother of nine grown children, grandmother of thirty-one grandchildren, and great-grandmother of seven. She received her BA in early childhood education from Idaho State University at the age of fifty-four and taught kindergarten for eight years. Since retirement, DeLoris has been active in the Idaho Writer's League, concentrating on family stories.

Sonja Herbert ("Letting the Light Shine") is the author of an award-winning, as yet unpublished novel about her mother surviving the Holocaust in a circus, and of many other true stories. Sonja presently lives in Germany, where she is doing research and getting reacquainted with her mother and siblings. Her website is *http://germanwriter.com*.

Ann Hite ("Believing in Magic") has published numerous short stories in publications such as *Plum Biscuit, Moonwort Review, A Cup of Comfort, Dead Mule*, and *Fiction Warehouse*. Her story titled "Surviving Mom" appeared in the second volume of Marlo Thomas's bestselling collection, *The Right Words at the Right Time*.

Patricia Hopper ("Christmas in the Rare Aul' Times") is a native of Dublin, Ireland, and lives in West Virginia. She earned both master's and bachelor's degrees in the arts from West Virginia University. Her fiction and nonfiction have appeared in magazines and anthologies. She credits her writing ability to her storytelling parents who made every family outing an experience.

Georgia A. Hubley ("Two Christmas Wishes") grew up in central Ohio. Currently, she and her husband live in Henderson, Nevada. Together, they have two grown sons; one resides in New York City, the other in Las Vegas. Georgia is a frequent contributor to the *Chicken Soup* series, as well as other anthologies, national magazines, and newspapers. Contact her at *GEOHUB@aol.com*.

Charlotte "Charlie" Hudson ("An Ocean Apart") was assigned to many locations overseas and in the United States during twenty-two years in the army. The Desert Storm veteran, now a freelance writer, lives with her husband, also a retired army officer, in South Florida.

Shannon Jacobyansky ("Tracking Twinkies") married her wonderful husband, Bill, seventeen years ago during the magical season of Christmas. God has since given them three beautiful gifts in their children Abraham, Ruth, and Samuel. No matter where they celebrate Christmas, you can be sure the bells and whistles of the Twinkie train will always be heard.

Jo Rae Johnson ("PJ Presents") is a freelance writer. Her two teens, Timothy and Lauren, have kept her seeing Christmas through a child's eyes. Jo Rae's stories have been included in the *365 Day Life Verse Devotional*, *Chicken Soup Series* (*Kids in the Kitchen* and *Tea Lover's Soul*), as well as *The Upper Room*. In addition to writing, Jo Rae enjoys tennis, gardening, and tea. She lives in Simpsonville, South Carolina, and can be reached at *t4me@bellsouth.net*.

Margaret Lang ("Recipe from Heaven") is a published author of thirty-five stories and full-time missionary to Africa with the Save the World Foundation, where she preaches the Gospel to school children, many with AIDS. She loves to tell stories to her three granddaughters via webcam and to anyone else who will listen.

Catherine Lanser ("Playing with Tradition") is a writer from Madison, Wisconsin. Her essays "The Great Walnut Caper" and "Forever Eighteen" have appeared in the Adams Media anthologies *Classic Christmas* and *Chick Ink*. Her essay, "The Smell of Lilacs," appears in *Stories of Strength*, an anthology to raise funds for Hurricane Katrina relief.

Angie Ledbetter ("Modern-Day Drummer Boy") is an author, freelance writer/editor, and columnist. She is a staff member of the *Rose & Thorn Literary e-zine* and a National Association of Women Writers Regional Representative. When not herding her three teenagers, she works on a fiction novel and writes poetry and magazine articles.

Naomi Levine ("The Seemingly Insignificant Present") is a retired French teacher whose work has appeared in numerous notable literary journals since 2003. In recent years, Naomi has had several poetry chapbooks published, including *Dancing on Silk Threads*, which placed second in the Shadow Poetry Chapbook Competition in 2007.

Patti Mattison Livingston ("Feast Day in Pharaoh Land") has always considered family and writing as her dual passions. Family came first; writing—a sporadic but determined activity—squeezed into the bustling days of rearing four children. Now widowed with grown children, Patti spends her time pouring words through her computer. She has been published in periodicals and in *Classic Christmas*.

Kevin Lynch ("The Autograph Collector") and his wife, JoAnn, live in St. Helena, California. Kevin is a freelance writer, and JoAnn is a flight attendant. Together, they like to cook, garden, and travel. This Christmas, Kevin's brother is bringing his family up from Australia, and according to Kevin, they won't be allowed to leave, until they sign the family poster!

Anne McCrady ("The Taste of Christmas") is a poet, storyteller, and motivational speaker whose writing is widely published. Among her credits are two award-winning poetry collections, an inspirational parable, and many oral narratives. More about her efforts to put "Words to Work for the Greater Good" can be found at her website, *www.InSpiritry.com.*

Linda Mehus-Barber ("No Wonder I Believe") lives with her loving husband, affectionately known as "the Buffalo," and their two dogs and cat, in the seaside community of Crescent Beach, in Surrey, British Columbia. When Linda is not teaching or writing, she loves to hike in the mountains or walk along the beach with her husband and dogs.

Edward L. Melin ("A Tradition Postponed") has lived more than ninety-five years of stories. He's conducted bands, taught music, and managed the Amarillo Symphony, while playing in its violin section. After the war, Edward returned to Texas, where he reared two children with his wife, Olive. They were married fifty years. Edward loves tennis but had to quit playing two years ago.

Amy Ammons Mullis ("Too Much Christmas") lives in upstate South Carolina, with a black Lab and a spoiled Dachshund, instead of a reindeer team. She works as a church secretary, but if she ever grows up, she hopes to live the adventurous life of an elf. Read more of her essays in *Letters to My Mother: Tributes to the Women Who Give Us Life—and Love*, and *A Cup of Comfort for Writers*.

David C. Nitz ("The Christmas Dance") presently serves as North Florida Evangelism Director for the Church of God. He also served seventeen years as a senior pastor in Englewood and in Tampa, Florida. David is a speaker, freelance writer, musician, and worship leader. He and his beloved wife, Amy, are the proud parents of three sons, Mike, James, and Phillip; two daughters-in-law, Leigh Ann and Bonnie; and grandchildren, Toby and Nigel.

Carol Nyman ("Honoring the Son" and "A Change of Attitude") has been writing nonfiction short stories for several years. She lives in Summerville, South Carolina, in a wonderful neighborhood, and works as a volunteer for autism research, family court issues, and other community organizations.

Heidi Lee Overson ("A Purposeful Journey") is an award-winning Wisconsin writer who lives in beautiful rural Coon Valley. She holds a technical communications degree, owns Lane Writing Company, and writes regularly for several local and national magazines. Heidi and her husband have four beautiful children and a small herd of Angora goats and llamas. They all live happily on their cozy Wisconsin hobby farm.

J. M. Pantatello ("Faux Santa") is retired and has been writing for several years. His stories have won awards in major contests and have been published in six anthologies, including *Classic Christmas*. He enjoys writing fantasy, mystery, and a little romance—to please his wife, Caroline. He is a member of the Long Island Writers' Guild and is editor of their newsletter.

Bill Pearsall ("The Guiding Star" and "A Family Tradition"), a former engineer, is currently employed as a high school math teacher. He and his wife, Jacque, have two daughters, Ashley and Sara; one son-in-law, David; and three granddaughters, Halsey, Harper, and Hillary. He has been a reader all his life and now enjoys writing as well. Bill credits his parents for his love of books.

Cheryl K. Pierson ("Maybe It's a Pony") lives in Oklahoma City with her husband. With many contributions to Adams Media books and *Chicken Soup* anthologies to her credit, she has also written six novels and is currently working on a screenplay adaptation of one of her manuscripts. She teaches writing classes and edits materials for other authors across the United States.

Connie Vigil Platt ("Happy Memories and Bright Futures") has finally realized her lifelong dream of becoming a published author. A number of her short stories have been published in national magazines including Dorchester Media. She was also published in *A Cup of Comfort for Weddings*. Her novel, *Pair a Dice*, can be found at all major bookstores.

Alissa Marie Polaski ("If You Believe in Magic"), the daughter of author/editor Helen Kay Polaski, has a bachelor's degree in Marketing and an associate's degree in Fashion Design. A native of Michigan, Alissa currently resides in Naples, Florida, where she works as an account executive and visual merchandiser for high-end home fashion.

Cappy Hall Rearick ("A Celluloid Christmas") is a humor columnist. Cappy has authored six columns: "Alive and Well in Hollywood," "Tidings," "Simply Southern," "Simply Senior," "Puttin' on the Gritz," and a monthly e-column called "Simply Something." She has three books in print: *Simply Southern, Simply Southern Ease*, and *Simply Christmas*. Cappy and her husband, Bill, live on St. Simons Island in Georgia.

Carol McAdoo Rehme ("Moon Flight") recently presented her adult children with their treasured childhood sleds—rescued from the sale of the family cabin. A freelance editor, author, and ghostwriter, she publishes prolifically in the inspirational market. Carol has coauthored seven books. Her latest is *Chicken Soup for the Empty Nester's Soul* (2008). You can contact Carol via e-mail at *carol@rehme.com* or through her website, *www.rehme.com*.

Stephen D. Rogers ("And Having a Ball") has had more than five hundred stories and poems selected to appear in more than two hundred publications. His website, *www.stephendrogers.com*, includes a list of new and upcoming titles as well as other timely information.

Sheila O'Brien Schimpf ("Wired") lives in East Lansing, Michigan, and is a former newspaper reporter who wrote a weekly column for thirteen years. She has won several writing prizes, teaches journalism occasionally at Michigan State University, and wants to publish a picture book. She also raises golden retrievers. Her three children have jobs (with health insurance) on the East and West Coasts, but they come home several times a year.

J. Troy Seate ("Messages in a Bottle") has been writing since surviving cancer surgery in 2001. He has written everything from novels to short stories to memoirs. He lives in Colorado and currently is working on a historical fiction that centers on mysterious property in the Golden area. Learn more about Troy's writing at *www.geocities .com/jtroyseate*.

Diane Serio ("Mrs. Claus") is an elementary school teacher by day and writer by night. Currently working on a novel and collections of short stories about teaching, she also has a collection of stories and poems with lessons learned from raising two wonderful boys, John and Jeremy.

Al Serradell ("The Photograph") is a recovering PR associate from Los Angeles, now residing in Oklahoma City. His work appears in several anthology books including the *Rocking Chair Reader* series, endorsed by Paul Harvey during his December 25, 2007, broadcast. Al also has a story in the Adams Media anthology *Christmas Through a Child's Eyes,* which was also endorsed by Paul Harvey.

Janet F. Smart ("The Old Santa Hat") lives in West Virginia, where she is a member of the Appalachian Wordsmiths. She and her husband, Charley, have three sons, Charley III, Andrew, and David. Janet inherited the ability to craft and sew from her mother and recently has begun writing stories and poems that focus on her family.

Joyce Stark ("Christmas Diaries") has just finished two books. One is about her travels in the United States and the other is a children's book. She explores a different area of the United States each year and claims it is "research" rather than pleasure, but no one believes her.

Jean Haynie Stewart ("Christmas Eve Luminaria") writes and edits from her Mission Viejo, California, home, which she shares with her husband of forty-eight years. Visits from her twin daughters and their families, including two grandchildren, allow her to spread her joy and love, and the meaning of Christmas, with them. Her stories can be found in numerous popular anthologies.

Donna Sundblad ("Santa's Call"), an author and full-time freelance writer, resides in Georgia with her husband, Rick. Among her published works you'll find *Pumping Your Muse*, a creative book for writers; *Windwalker*, a young adult fantasy novel; and various inspirational short stories and articles. Check her website for more information at *www.theinkslinger.net*.

Terri Tiffany ("Silver Linings") counseled adults for almost twenty years before opening a Christian bookstore. She now resides in Florida, with her husband, where she writes full-time. Her stories have appeared in numerous anthologies, Sunday school take-home papers, and women's magazines. She also writes inspirational romance books. Please e-mail her at *terri.tiffany@yahoo.com*.

Anna von Reitz ("The Gift of Knowledge") is a journalist and public relations specialist living in Big Lake, Alaska. Anna became interested in writing as a college student and has pursued her muse ever since. She has just finished her first full-length novel.

Suzanne Waring ("The Advent Calendar") lives in Great Falls, Montana, with her husband. After a thirty-year career as a teacher/administrator for a two-year college, she has turned her attention to freelance writing. She has contributed to *Mature Years* magazine and *Classic Christmas: True Stories of Holiday Cheer and Goodwill* anthology. During the past year, the *Great Falls Tribune* has printed sixteen of her articles in its *50Plus* supplement.

Laura S. White ("The Special Box") lives in rural Michigan with three cats. She enjoys spending time in, and writing about, her two-room cabin in the north woods. Her faith keeps her strong and her memories keep her fulfilled. Laura dedicates this story to the memory of her mother, whose place at the table now remains empty.

Junette Kirkham Woller ("The Mirror Pond") has a background in fine and performing arts and journalism. Her work has appeared in newspapers, magazines, newsletters, church bulletins, poetry collections, and books: *Chocolate for a Teen's Soul*, *Quotable Texas Women*, and *Summer Shorts*. Future publications containing her work are *Memory Bridge* and *Sweet Dreams*.

About the Editor

Helen Szymanski and her high school sweetheart, Thomas Polaski, have been married for thirty-three years and have three grown children of whom they are very proud.

Helen, who also writes as Helen Kay Polaski, has authored eight books for Adams Media and is also a frequent contributor to a variety of anthologies.

Over the course of her career, Helen has progressed from poet to essayist, photojournalist to author, and newspaper editor to book editor. As an enjoyable pastime, Helen keeps the magic of her own childhood traditions alive through her website *www.theelfdoor.com* where she and her husband design elf doors, a hobby she began when she was eight years old. Contact her at *hkpolaski@yahoo.com*.